COACHING MATCH-UP DEFENSE:
By The Experts

Edited by
Bob Murrey

COACHES CLINICS

COACHES
CHOICE™

ISBN: 1-58518-335-0
Library of Congress Catalog Card Number: 2001095166

Front cover photo: Tom Hauck/Allsport
Cover design: Kerry Hartjen
Book layout: Jennifer Bokelmann

Coaches Choice
P.O. Box 1828
Monterey, CA 93942
http://www.coacheschoice.com

Additional information on either the USA Coaches Clinic schedule or the USA Coaches library can be obtained by either calling 1-800-COACH-13 or faxing 1-314-991-1929.

Throughout this book, the masculine shall be deemed to include the feminine and vice versa.

CONTENTS

DIAGRAM LEGEND

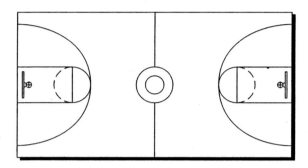

PLAYERS

(5) Centers

(3, 4) Forwards

(1, 2) Guards

◯ = Offense

X = Defense

⊙ = Player with the Ball

– – → = Direct Pass

⟶⊣ = Screen

〰→ = Dribble

⟶ = Cut of Player with or without the Ball

╫╫╫╫→ = Shot

CHAPTER 1

AMOEBA DEFENSE

JIM BOLLA

DIAGRAM 1-1.

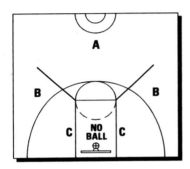

First we break the court down into four areas; A, B, C, and in the lane — the *no ball* area. This is basically a 1-3-1 set with different rules for different players in different areas.

DIAGRAM 1-2.

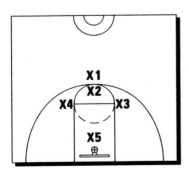

X1 and X2 are the guards, and they will play *tandem*. X3 and X4 will start at the elbows. Always put your best rebounder on the left side facing the basket because most teams are right oriented. Your best athlete is X5.

DIAGRAM 1-3.

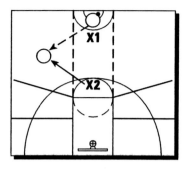

The guards can extend out to half-court. They can run and jump, push the ball to the side, etc. When there is a pass, X2 takes the ball and X1 drops and defends in the post area.

DIAGRAM 1-4.

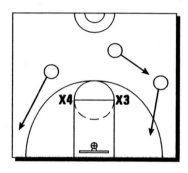

X3 will have the left hand and foot up and will force the ball to the side. If the ball is on the wing, X3 pushes the ball to the corner. We always push the ball toward the baseline. X4 has the right hand up, right foot up, and will do likewise.

DIAGRAM 1-5.

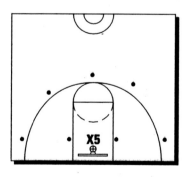

X5's responsibility is to *be in line* with the ball.

DIAGRAM 1-6.

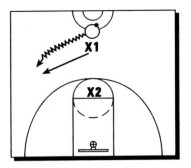

Anytime the ball is dribbled, X1 stays with the ball. X2 remains in the post area.

DIAGRAM 1-7.

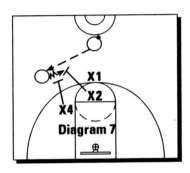

If the ball had been passed to the side and X2 was guarding and then the ball was dribbled back to the top, X2 would stay with the ball.

DIAGRAM 1-8.

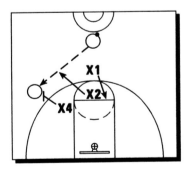

If the ball is passed to the wing, X4 will come out to push the ball to the corner. X1 will drop. X2 can hedge out for the return pass.

DIAGRAM 1-9.

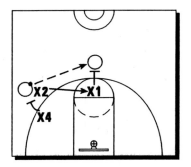

Sometimes we run a *double team* with X4 and X2. X1 is in the post area. If the ball is passed back, X1 will take the ball, but not until he sees that X2 is covering the post area. If X1 leaves too early, the ball can be passed into the post. Our philosophy is that anytime the ball is moving sideways or backwards, *we will not attack it.*

DIAGRAM 1-10.

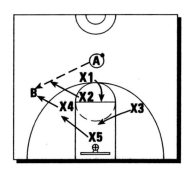

If A passes to B on the wing, X4 comes out and plays it. X2 hedges out, X1 plays the high post, X5 is on the ballside low, and X3 is in the middle.

DIAGRAM 1-11.

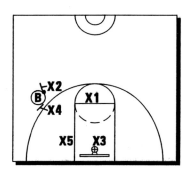

X2 can either trap with X4, or harass. X5 is on the low block, X3 in the paint.

DIAGRAM 1-12.

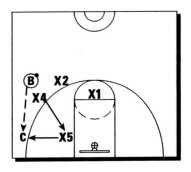

If the ball goes into the corner where we want it to go, X5 takes the ball in the corner. X4 actually *cross-steps* back into the post area.

It is very important that the right hand and foot are up because when the pass goes to the corner, the rule is to cross over and step into the low post area. If you come out the other way, there is a tendency to turn the back on the ball. X4 will *maintain sight* of the ball, and depending on your choice, X4 will be in full front or half front on the low post. X5 must play the ball.

DIAGRAM 1-13.

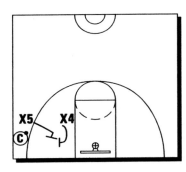

X5 will play on the upside of the ball. In the Amoeba, you give up the baseline. We want to *force* the offensive player to go *baseline* so that we can *trap*. X4 will set the trap with X5.

DIAGRAM 1-14.

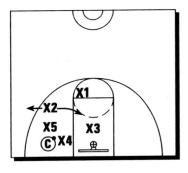

X2 can be in deny, or X2 can stay in on the post. We will give the pass back to the top. We call this the *umbrella*. This is effective because most people assume that if you beat X5 on the baseline, you will get a basket. But we are trapping with X4.

DIAGRAM 1-15.

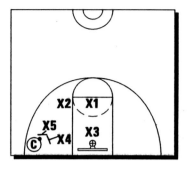

This takes a lot of people by surprise as they are driving. If X1 and X2 are in, and the ball is passed out, many times you will get a deflection by your guards. The *no ball area* is covered.

DIAGRAM 1-16.

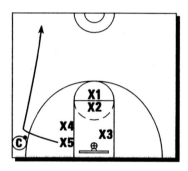

If C had the ball and X5 saw that C was going to shoot, we will always *run past the shooter*. As C is taking the jump shot, X5 runs by and *buttonhooks.* Most of the time we will get the rebound. If we get the re-bound, X5 releases. That's why we want X5 to be our best athlete.

DIAGRAM 1-17.

You *buttonhook* because if they didn't take the shot, X4 and X5 can still *trap.*

DIAGRAM 1-18.

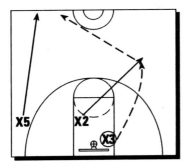

But many times the shot would be taken, rebounded by X3, passed to X2 and then to X5 for the layup.

DIAGRAM 1-19.

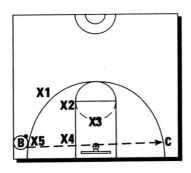

If the ball is in the corner, X5 is on the ball, X4 in the low post, X3 in the lane, X1 is out on the denial, and B makes a skip-pass to C.

DIAGRAM 1-20.

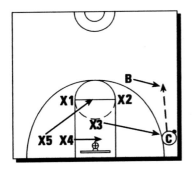

In this situation, X3 would become X5. X4 is in the middle, X5 is on the wing. X3 would be *on the ball.* That's the only time your back line will change. When the ball is passed from C to B, X2 takes the ball and X1 remains in the high post.

DIAGRAM 1-21.

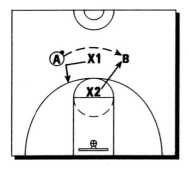

We drill the move between X1 and X2. As the ball is passed between A and B, X1 and X2 must *communicate*. The word is "*go*." As A passes to B, X2 remains at the high post until X1 says "go."

DIAGRAM 1-22.

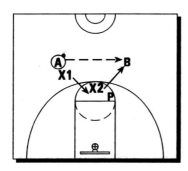

Then, we drill it with a post player.

DIAGRAM 1-23.

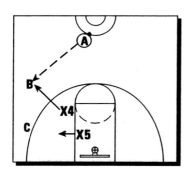

This drill is for the *big people*. As A passed to B, X4 took the ball and X5 was ready to cover C.

DIAGRAM 1-24.

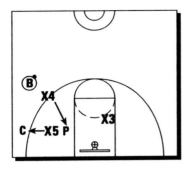

As the ball is passed from B to C, X5 covers C and X4 drops back to take the low post. X4 must use the crossover step. It is important that you swing the arm and leg in the crossover move. You *create the illusion*. It looks as if the post is open and that it will be guarded by X3. However, X4 will get there to intercept. We use the three-point line as the farthest out we want our players to go. In practice, you will find out which players have the quickness to get back and cover the low post from the wing.

DIAGRAM 1-25.

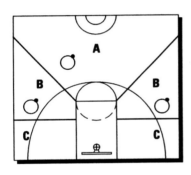

Another drill is used when we have the areas drawn on the floor. The coach says which area the ball is in and the five defensive players adjust. For example, B to C, and the *zone must shift*.

DIAGRAM 1-26.

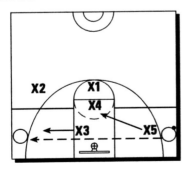

One of the toughest is when the ball went from C to C. X4 then became X5 and took the corner, and X5 was the offside wing. This drill is done without the ball. It gets the players to *think*.

DIAGRAM 1-27.

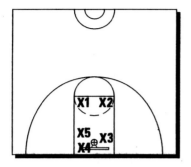

If the coach said *no ball*, then all five players collapsed into the lane. We didn't care if they passed it back out. We wanted it to go back out; it gave us time to *regroup*. Now let's extend this. You can play this as a half-court trap or a full-court defense. If you have great guards, they can harass people and the back men can actually rest.

DIAGRAM 1-28.

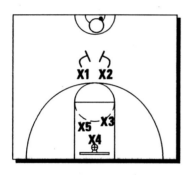

You can have X1 and X2 up, and they can *trap*.

DIAGRAM 1-29.

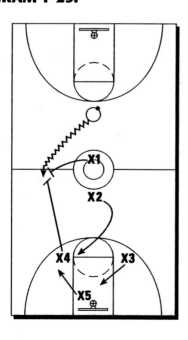

You can play it so that if the ball is dribbled to the right, X1 and X4 will *run and jump*.

DIAGRAM 1-30.

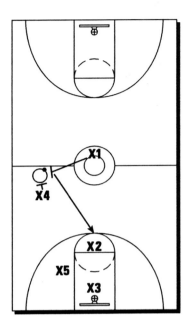

We ran a *jump switch*. X2 would be in the high-post area, X3 in the paint, X5 on the side of the ball.

DIAGRAM 1-31.

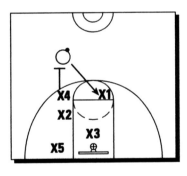

X1 drops back to the weakside elbow area. X1 and X4 could also *double-team*.

DIAGRAM 1-32.

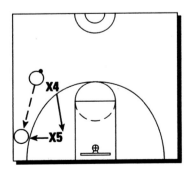

If the ball is passed to the corner, X5 takes the ball and X4 takes the low post. This is the same concept but X4 has a long way to go.

DIAGRAM 1-33.

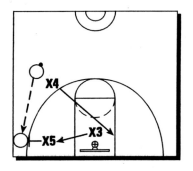

If X4 can't get there, we run the X move. X3 will come over and take the low post and X4 will take *weakside*.

DIAGRAM 1-34.

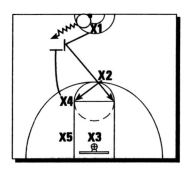

Again, if X4 is our better wing player, X4 would come up and take the ball. X1 will drop to the weakside elbow. X2 goes with the flow into the high-post area. We would tell X1 to *hide*.

DIAGRAM 1-35.

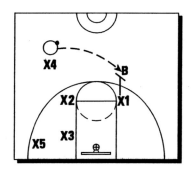

If the offense picks up the dribble, X5 is in position to cover the corner, X3 is in the low post, X2 cuts off the passing lanes, and we actually have our X1 player to *get down and hide*. What happens is that B seems open and X1 can *make the steal*.

DIAGRAM 1-36.

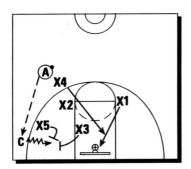

If the ball is passed to C in the corner, X5 will drive him to the baseline for the trap with X3. X4 can't get to the baseline from that far out, so X4 goes to the *weakside rebounding position.* Always protect the *"no ball"* area. X1 will cover low until X4 gets there. X2 is still in the high-post area.

We do give them an open diagonal pass, but we would rather have that than give them the ball inside. Understand that when the player dribbles the baseline, he thinks he is going to get a shot. It's not so easy to make that diagonal pass. Many times X4 will get the interception of that diagonal pass.

DIAGRAM 1-37.

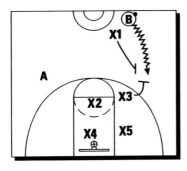

Now the other side. When X1 pushes the ball left, X1 and X3 will *double-team* every time.

DIAGRAM 1-38.

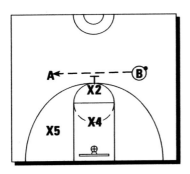

X5 cuts off the corner, X4 is in the lane, and A looks open. X2 can intercept that pass. X2 never leaves the post area until the ball is in the air.

DIAGRAM 1-39.

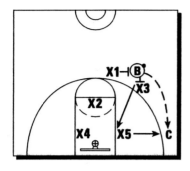

If the pass goes to the corner, X5 comes out and X3 makes the *crossover step* and covers the low post. This is the same coverage as the other side. X5 doesn't leave the low-post player until X3 can cover that spot.

DIAGRAM 1-40.

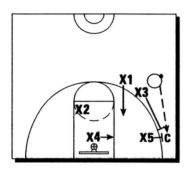

A variation is to have X3 trap with X5 in the corner and X4 take the low post. This is usually a *scout situation*.

DIAGRAM 1-41.

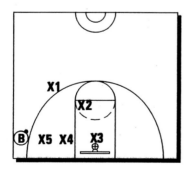

We got to the point that whenever the ball went on the right side of the floor. We went *man-to-man*. So, we started off in a half-court trap with a jump switch, but if the ball went into the corner, we played man-to-man until the ball was dead. Now, let's take this full court. There are five ways you break a full-court press. You have a 1-4 set. You inbound the ball to your best ball handler and you clear four people out of the area. You have a 2-3 set with two guards bringing it up. You have a 3-2 set, a 4-1, and a 5-0. The nice thing about the *Amoeba* is that the more people involved in a half-court situation when they are breaking a press, the better it is for the Amoeba. The hardest thing to defend is the 1-4 set.

DIAGRAM 1-42.

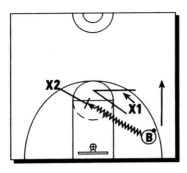

DIAGRAM 1-43.

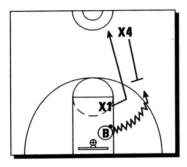

Against a 1-4, we will *run and jump* with the guards. We never want to get beat up the sideline. The same rules are established for the full-court as in the half-court trap.

On the run and jump, X1 must drop at a 45-degree angle. We want the ball to move so that we can jump it again. When you have very good guards who work well together, they can really harass the offense. Anytime that the dribbler turned his back, we would try to come up from the blind side for the *steal or double-team.* So, against a 1-4 set, you go two guards up and establish a 45-degree angle for the run and jump. If the ball handler is weak, fake, and if the dribbler picks up his dribble, go into a *deny.*

Diagram 1-43: X4 can run and jump or double. We point at the ball, and we point at the man in your area, *establish the triangle.*

DIAGRAM 1-44.

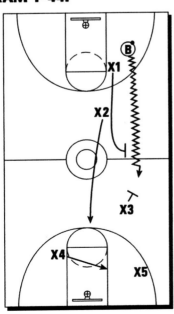

If they run on the side of X3, it is automatic. X1 and X3 will trap. We use the half-court line as the trap area so they can't throw the ball back.

Sometimes we will let B think that he is beating us up the sideline. The faster they go, the more out of control they go, and the better this defense becomes. As the ball goes up the sideline and X3 comes to trap, X2 drops down, X4 comes down into the lane. X5 is playing ballside. If the ball is reversed, X2 can be in a position to help.

DIAGRAM 1-45.

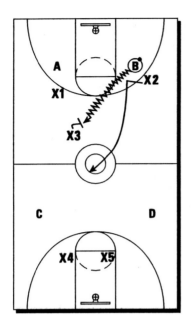

With a two-guard set, we have X3 play center field. We want to establish a left or right orientation. Any side-to-side movement is a *jump switch* between X1 and X2. If we can bring the ball into the middle, we will jump switch with X3 and X2. X1 drops to line of ball.

DIAGRAM 1-46.

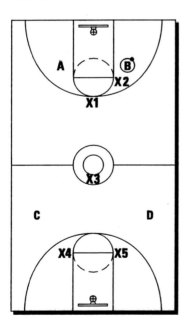

If B has the ball, we aren't going to play A. X1 is going to drop at a 45-degree angle and try for an X1-X2 jump switch.

DIAGRAM 1-47.

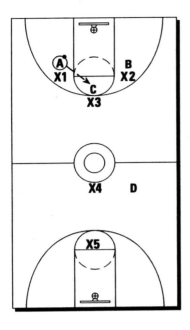

If they bring three people up, A, B, and C, we will bring X3 up. The same rules prevail. If the ball goes from A to C, X1 and X2 drop down and we are back in our *45-degree angle off the ball. Create the triangle defensively.*

DIAGRAM 1-48. DRILL

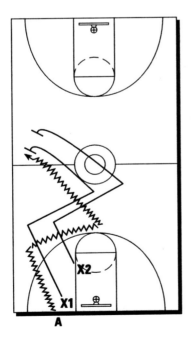

We start off with a basic zigzag stance drill. Then we will work on trapping with A on offense and X1 and X2 on defense. A zigzags and X1 and X2 run a *jump switch* and go about 10 feet over the half-court line and then trap. This eliminates the backcourt. Whether we are in full-court or half-court situations, we want the trap in the front court.

DIAGRAM 1-49.

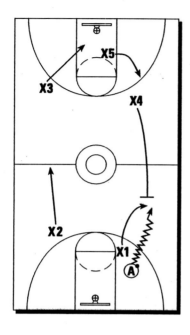

We tell our kids that there is an invisible line down the middle of the floor. If the ball is going this way, defensively our *rotation* is always this way. So, if the ball is on your side of the floor and coming toward you, you will never be wrong if you are *attacking the next player in line.*

DIAGRAM 1-50.

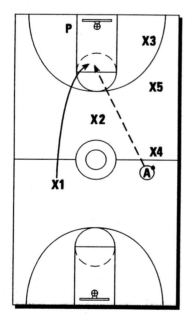

Sometimes we get this alignment with X1 coming back into the lane. Many times A thinks he sees P open on the post. As the pass is thrown, X1 comes into the passing lane and intercepts. We have been successful in creating the illusion that the post is open.

You must teach your guards to stay on their side of the floor and not to chase the ball laterally. If the ball is reversed, we have the same philosophy. We just change directions and come to meet the next player on the ballside. When the ball advances, we come to meet it. When the ball goes from side to side, we just make adjustments laterally. It really deflates a team when they think they have beaten your trap and you intercept a pass by creating the illusion. If you are going to use this, you must go over it every day and make sure your players know their limitations. And you must adjust this defense according to their limitations.

CHAPTER 2

MATCHING UP
FROM THE 1-1-3
Lou Campanelli

We do not call this defense a zone. We do not want the players to get in what I call a zone mentality. I don't want them thinking that they are just defending an area on the court.

DIAGRAM 2-1.

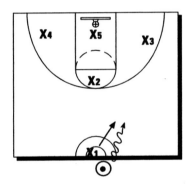

X1 picks up the dribbler at mid-court. We want to be strong down the middle, so X2 stays there and prevents any *quick pass* into the post. X1 stays with the dribbler until he almost gets to the wing position.

DIAGRAM 2-2.

The first pass is to the wing. X3 must take the ball. X2 gets to the ballside elbow, X1 drops to the weakside elbow. X5 fronts the post. X4 slides across. You must decide how much of the floor you can cover with this defense. The quicker the team, the more area they can cover. I believe that in high school you don't have to go out farther than 18' - 20'. When you are guarding the man with the ball, say, *"Ball."* Never have two people guarding the person with the ball. You can't play a matchup defense with two players on the ball.

DIAGRAM 2-3.

Never allow the ball to split two defenders.

DIAGRAM 2-4.

X3 is pressuring the ball. It is critical to have both elbows covered. X5 fronts the post, or a hard 3/4 position. He can't play behind because on the pass to the corner, X5 must cover it. The wing passes to the corner and X5 takes the corner. X4 covers ball-side box. X3 makes the long slide to the baseline on the weakside. X1 helps back until X3 gets there, then X1 recovers. Which way does X4 go, high or low? I don't know. We just tell him to get there to take away the direct pass into the post.

DIAGRAM 2-5.

The ball comes out from the corner. X2 has the first pass out of the corner. X1 goes to ballside elbow. What kills a zone is the *indecision* as to who is going to cover the ball. You don't cover an *area*, you *cover a man in the area*.

DIAGRAM 2-6.

When the ball is reversed from the wing to the point, and then to the other wing, X1 comes out to take the ball when it is at the point. X1 knows that he has the first pass back to the top. X2 drops back to the elbow. As the pass is made from the point to the wing, X2 continues to the other elbow and X1 drops back to the weakside elbow. X3 is cheating toward the wing, making eye contact with the offense. X3 knows that the first pass to the wing is his. X4 fronts the post, and X5 is in the lane.

DIAGRAM 2-7.

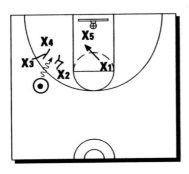

X3's closeout is as tough as any. X3 can't run all the way. X3 sprints part of the way, but when he gets close, he breaks down with short steps and his hand up. On this side of the court, I prefer the left foot up. X3's weight should be back. Don't allow penetration. If the ball is allowed to be dribbled toward the elbow area, that will hurt. If X3 is beaten on this dribble, X2 attacks and must stop the ball immediately. Wing-to-elbow penetration will kill you. The elbow area is the heart of the defense. X3 and X2 can trap if the dribble is toward the elbow area. If the dribble is to the corner, X3 can play it man-to-man.

DIAGRAM 2-8.

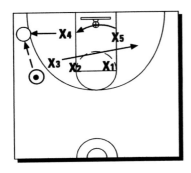

Suppose the wing passes to the corner. X4 will cover the corner, X5 will front, X3 will make the long slide. X1 and X2 cover the elbows. When you are going to trap, the natural thing for players to do is to run over and then put their hands up. A great teaching point is to run over with their hands up.

DIAGRAM 2-9. "RED"

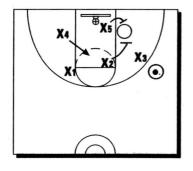

In the match-up, you must have several calls to cover certain situations. This is the call for X2 to *double down* on the low post. X3 is covering the ball on the wing. Many post players can't pass well. When the ball goes into the post, as the ball is in the air, X2 is coming. We want to trap so that the post cannot pass out to the *weakside*. We keep him from *turning middle*. We will give up the turn to the baseline. He must shoot over the defense and it takes him away from the board. X3 denies the pass back out. X1 drops and anticipates a pass back out on top. X4 also is an interceptor. When you are in the trap on the pivot, don't go for the steal. Get your *hands up*. The official is right there on the baseline. The steals come from X1, X3, and X4. Don't let the post put the ball on the floor and don't let him *turn to the middle*.

DIAGRAM 2-10.

Suppose that X1 shoots the passing lane but gets there late and can't get it.

DIAGRAM 2-11.

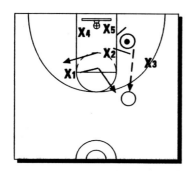

This causes an *"X Move."* X1 takes the ball and X2 fills the weakside elbow.

Question: Who gets the first pass out from the corner if X3 makes the long slide?

DIAGRAM 2-12.

Answer: X2 is responsible for the *first pass out*. X1 will take the near elbow.

DIAGRAM 2-13.

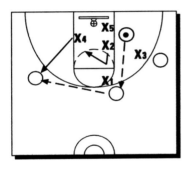

This is a *slide* for the more experienced team. The ball comes out of the post and is then passed to the weakside wing. X1 took the first pass out of the post and X4 is responsible for the pass to the wing. X2 starts out but sees X4 already moving and so X2 drops back on the baseline.

DIAGRAM 2-14. "BLUE"

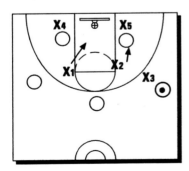

The *short corner* always gives zones problems. An offensive player filled the short corner from the weakside. X5 can't cover it because you expose the post. X4 must go with the cutter. X1 slides back to help, X2 pinches into the middle.

DIAGRAM 2-15.

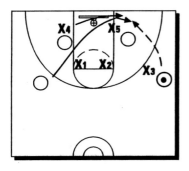

From scouting reports you would know who would be the cutter. If the wing goes to the short corner, it is the same move by X4.

DIAGRAM 2-16.

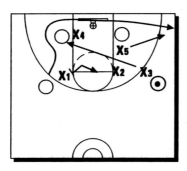

If the wing goes to the deep corner and the ball is passed there from the wing, X3 makes the long slide as before. X5 will go to the deep corner. X4 must communicate with X5 and tell him the cutter is coming. X4 then takes the nearside block.

DIAGRAM 2-17.

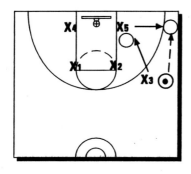

Sometimes, as a *change-up*, you can use the *short slide*. X5 will take the corner man and X3 will drop to the near post.

DIAGRAM 2-18.

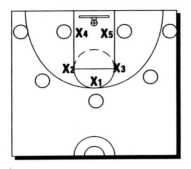

A great drill to use with this defense is to play 7 vs. 5. The defense must anticipate the next pass. You must work hard in this defense.

Question: If X4 is up on the ball and the ball goes to the corner, who covers it?

DIAGRAM 2-19.

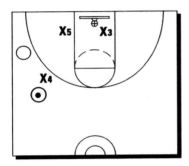

Answer: X5 takes the corner and X3 covers ballside post.

DIAGRAM 2-20.

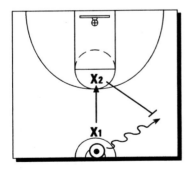

Another teaching point is the gray area when X1 picks up the dribbler at mid-court. If the pass is rather short, X2 may come out and take it and X1 will drop back into the middle.

DIAGRAM 2-21.

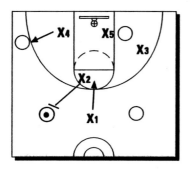

Against a 2-1-2. X1 and X2 must communicate, if X1 is out, X2 is in. If X2 comes out, then X1 is in.

We have designed this defense so that X5 doesn't have to come out and guard the high-post area.

CHAPTER 3

THE MATCH-UP DEFENSE

JOE CIAMPI

When you design a *game-like drill*, you can't stop them every 10 seconds; you don't correct every 10 seconds, etc. You set a time limit and you have winners and losers. You discuss why they won, and you reward them in some way.

We use *three picture words* in every one of our defensive drills: *delay, disrupt, and deflect*. We want to *delay* the dribbler anywhere on the floor. We want to be able to *deflect* every pass to the inside. We want to *disrupt* the shot.

Some people say *"contest the shot."* We want to disrupt the shot and disrupt the offensive pattern. I must get my players to understand the *concepts*. I want my players, to *create* the action, rather than be reactors, so we run a lot of *traps*. We run *traps* off the dribble or off the pass. Don't *react, create. Trap* the ball, overplay. When we trap, two people will be *trappers*; two people will be *stealers*, and one person will be the *safety*.

DIAGRAM 3-1.

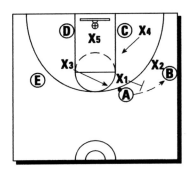

The ball is passed from A to B. X2 is on the ball. On the pass, X1 and X2 will trap; X3 and X4 become stealers; X5 is the safety. The only thing we are giving you is the *cross-court pass*. If B would start dribbling, X1 and X2 stay with the dribbler. X3 and X4 will adjust, and X5 will stay in the lane. The trap is a basic part of the match-up. So, how do we work on that?

DIAGRAM 3-2.

A is near center court. X1 and X2 are in a position to trap. A has 10 seconds in which to handle the ball and can go anywhere she wants. X1 and X2 will work on the trap, containment. When I say, *"Time,"* A passes to B; X1 and X2 will react and run to the center of the floor, and B will try to dribble in the other direction versus X1 and X2. If A picks up the dribble, X1 and X2 try to take away the high-post pass. Just what is the match-up?

We want to obtain more rebounds than our opponents, that's the key. Shooting percentage is a big thing to us. *Match-up* is ball pressure and four people taking away inside passes. Everyone is not a great shooter. We give certain people shots.

DIAGRAM 3-3.

This is the area where the least amount of shots are taken against us. We very seldom defend that area after the entry.

DIAGRAM 3-4.

The ball is at the wing and the ball is passed to the corner. We have a *"cutoff situation."* When the ball goes to the corner, X4 attacks the ball. X2 makes a *backslide* and covers the block. When the pass comes back from C to B, X2 covers the wing rather than chasing out to the point. We are more concerned with the pass going inside than with the person at the top. We have a *rotating zone* with man-to-man goals.

DIAGRAM 3-5.

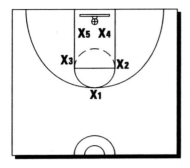

We like to show a *1-2-2* set. X1 has her heels on the top of the key. X2 is the other guard. X3 is two steps below the elbow. Eighty percent of the time the ball will go to the right side, and her move is to cover the *weakside block*. X4 is the top inside player and should be able to be replaced. Or else you should play your top inside player in the X3 position. X5 must play a lot of *hard-nosed* defense on the inside. I do not play my top inside scorer at the X5 position.

DIAGRAM 3-6.

You can also do a *1-1-3* set by moving X3 back and X2 over.

DIAGRAM 3-7.

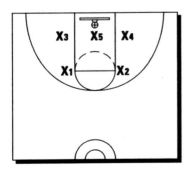

You can go *2-3* by moving X1 to the other elbow.

DIAGRAM 3-8.

If we are in a *1-1-3*, on a pass to the wing, X2 takes the first pass to either side. If you run the guards in tandem, it takes away the pass to the high post. It is also a great *trapping defense*.

DIAGRAM 3-9.

Let's get back to the *1-2-2* and discuss X1, X2, and X3. The ball goes from A to B. X2's job is to delay the pass from B into the block area. You just can't say *take away* the inside. We want them to *delay* that pass. If they make a bounce pass or a lob pass, you have done your job. X2's first rule is that she cannot take more than *three slides*. She must not overextend. She cannot go beyond the three-point line. When X2 is out there, X2 must have her head on the *ball shoulder*.

DIAGRAM 3-10.

If the ball is at the top of the key, X2 and X3 must take away the inside passing lanes. The *inside arm*, closest to the lane, must be out at *shoulder level*. When the ball goes from A to B, X2 should be on B when the ball is caught. X1 will be at *ball elbow*, and X3 will be in line with the ball and the opposite corner, one foot in the lane.

DIAGRAM 3-11.

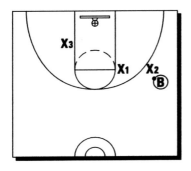

When B has the ball, X2 is on the ball shoulder; X1 at ball elbow, and X3 on that line with one foot in the lane. If the pass were made to the other wing, that situation would be mirrored. When the ball goes from point to wing, X2 pivots and then does a *"push and glide."* If B dribbles instead of passing, we have a *cut-off* step. If B dribbles, the first step of our defensive player is back. Push off with the front foot. The defensive player must make some room so the dribbler can be stopped without committing the foul. So, one step back, two over, and on the second step, the defensive player should make contact.

DIAGRAM 3-12. X-OUT SERIES

This is a two-part drill. A and B both have their outside foot on the block. C and D are off the court waiting. A rolls the ball to the foul line. A picks it up with her back to the basket. B makes a *lateral slide* across the lane and then approaches A. A pivots and B plays defense. A shoots; B contests the shot, boxes out, and goes to the ball. We do that for two minutes. If A gets the rebound, she continues to shoot; if B gets the rebound the drill is over.

DIAGRAM 3-13. "COMBO"

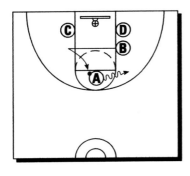

A gets no more than *two dribbles*. We tell A which way we want her to go. Same rules as on the last one. When A dribbles, B takes the cutoff step, and two steps over. Don't block the shot; let A shoot the ball. B blocks out. We work on cutting off, contesting the shot. If A makes the shot, B has five push-ups; if B gets the rebound, A has five push-ups.

Spend more time *praising* the good performer rather than the poor performer. I once had a player who was a good defensive player and never made a mistake. I praised her and said, "She's a pirate." I said that she is the only one on the team who can steal the ball well. Another player came to me and asked what she had to do to become a pirate. From that instance, I have given permission to certain players to go after the ball handler.

In the *X-Out Series*, we are working on *shot contesting, rebounding, don't foul the jump shooter* outside of the paint.

DIAGRAM 3-14.

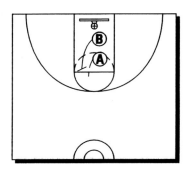

For the post people, A is near the basket and B is directly behind her. A has the ball. A will toss the ball out and run out and catch the ball with her back to the basket. B will come out right behind and *"belly up"* to A. We want B to make contact with her upper legs. A pivots; B slides and keeps her verticality. When A shoots, B contests the shot, then boxes out. In the paint, we *hit and hold*. Outside the paint we hit and go to the ball.

DIAGRAM 3-15.

At another basket, we will have the wing people either tossing the ball out or rolling the ball to the three-point line and playing one-on-one. This is a two-minute drill. Remember, from our match-up, we want to *rebound, take away* the inside, and *contest* every shot.

DIAGRAM 3-16.

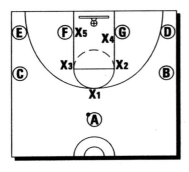

We have seven offensive people. We want to put *pressure* on the ball and take away the inside. A has the ball. X1 has her heels at the top of the key. X1's job is to get the ball to the side and delay the pass down the middle. X2 is at the elbow with her inside hand and arm at shoulder level. X3 is two steps below the elbow with her inside arm at shoulder level. X4 and X5 are inside in the lane. X4 and X5 are a step above F and G and side-guarding them. We want to show the offense that we are not playing a zone. So, X4 and X5 will have the foot and arm *closest* to the ball in front of F and G.

DIAGRAM 3-17.

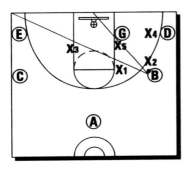

A passes to B. We should be in another position. No more than *three slides*. Don't overextend. We are taking away the inside. Overplay the best shooters. When B catches the ball, X2 is there, one foot on the three-point line with her head on the ballside. X4 moves halfway to the corner by going above G. X4 steps in front of G and opens up. X5 replaces X4. X5 must be in line with the ball and the basket. X3 is in line with the ball and the opposite corner, one foot in the paint. X1 drops to the ballside elbow.

DIAGRAM 3-18.

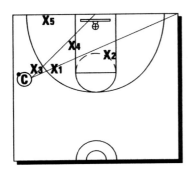

This is mirrored on the other side of the floor.

DIAGRAM 3-19.

C passes to D in the corner. We call this *"Fire."* We *create* the action. X4 takes the ball; X2 fronts the post; X5 drops to the middle even with the basket; X1 denies the return pass, and X3 is in the lane weakside. We want that to be *wide open*; X3 can deflect the pass and score.

DIAGRAM 3-20.

If D passes to B and B passes back to the middle, by that time, X2 comes up in the middle and she becomes the point.

DIAGRAM 3-21.

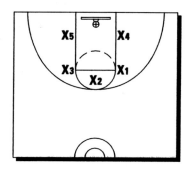

This puts us in our basic *match-up*. When the ball goes from the wing to the corner, we *create* the action. We are going to play five defensive people against three offensive people and rebound five people. We let one of the offensive players shoot the ball from the outside, then take away your inside and your best shooter on the outside.

DIAGRAM 3-22.

Suppose the offense has a high post and a low post. A, B, and C are on the perimeter. A has passed to B. X2 has her head on the *ballside* of B. X4 is halfway to the corner, but if no one is in the corner, she steps back in. X5 is on a line between the ball and the basket, and X3 is on the line between the ball and the corner. X1 fronts the high post. We won't play the high post with X5 unless she catches the ball.

DIAGRAM 3-23.

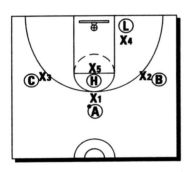

If we see you strictly going high-low, we use *"21 tandem."* We match-up and play you man-to-man on the high-low and everyone else plays the zone. We like it when you take your post people *away* from the basket.

DIAGRAM 3-24.

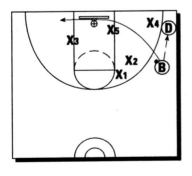

If B passes to D and then cuts through, we let you go if you are going away from the ball. X2 will drop two steps and then take the person who is replacing B.

DIAGRAM 3-25.

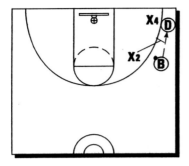

We can also use *"crush."* This means that on the B to D pass, X2 will trap with X4. *Crush* means that the person on the ball goes with the pass.

DIAGRAM 3-26.

This can also occur when the pass goes from the point to the wing. We trap the first pass with X1 and X2. You must get your kids to believe what we have defensively will *create* opportunities for us.

The drills should be time-related, and *goal-related*. When we leave the locker room, the last thing that they will see are *three statements. Ball pressure*. We want the ball pressured at all times. *Take away the inside*. Take away the inside with the arms first. X2 and X3 will have the inside arms shoulder high in the lane. X4 and X5 will have both arms shoulder high. Take away the passing lanes with your arms; you take away the dribble penetration with the body. *Rebound*. We want you to rebound the blocks.

DIAGRAM 3-27.

When the ball is passed from A to B, *move* when the ball moves. X3 slides to the three-point line. X5 goes halfway to the corner. X4 will be in line with the ball and the basket. X2 will be in line with the ball and the corner. X1 will take ballside elbow. X3 exerts ball pressure. X3's head is on the *ball shoulder*. If B switches the ball from one shoulder to the other, X3 doesn't step over. She switches hands and mirrors the ball.

DIAGRAM 3-28. 30-SECOND DRILL

A and B are 15' apart. C is in the middle. Hold the ball for a *two-count*. C mirrors the ball. No lob passes.

DIAGRAM 3-29.

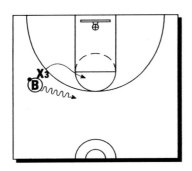

On the dribble, X3 makes a *cutoff* step and slides over.

DIAGRAM 3-30.

When the ball is passed from the point to the wing to the corner, you can play it different ways. You can play it *"normal."*

DIAGRAM 3-31.

You can *"Fire."* X2 replaces X5, and X5 drops across the lane; X3 goes to the ball-side elbow; X1 denies the return pass. X5 is in a position to rebound, and X2 fronts the high post.

DIAGRAM 3-32.

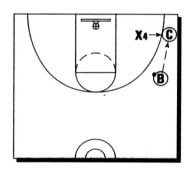

X4 must have the inside arm up shoulder level to take away the inside. When the pass is made, X4 must move on the pass. When X4 comes out, she has her hands above her head. X4 runs two-thirds of the way, and then comes under control and *closes out.*

We are really playing a *sagging* man-to-man. She's taking away the passing lane and the shot. If C is a good shooter, *close in.* Stop the shot. If she goes baseline, we are going to try to *jam* you on the baseline. X4's job is to stop the shot first. X4 gets help on the dribble. *Close in* on great shooters. Make them put the ball on the floor.

DIAGRAM 3-33.

The players run back to their original positions. Now the drill is run on the other side. The same rules apply. If X3 shoots a three-point shot and makes it, her team gets three points. The scoring is three points for a three-point shot, two points for a two, two points for a rebound, and three points for a put-back.

DIAGRAM 3-34.

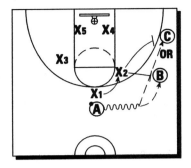

X3 shoots and misses and X2 gets the rebound. Someone must play the ball. C will take X3 and they will play 3-on-3.

DIAGRAM 3-35.

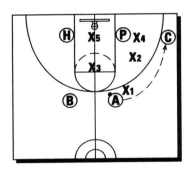

When these six players finish, the next six are up.

DIAGRAM 3-36.

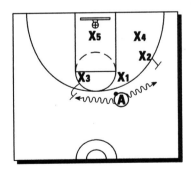

Now we do the drill with a shot from the wing.

DIAGRAM 3-37.

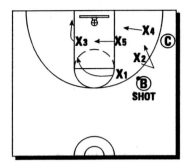

When the ball is in the corner, the back leg of X2 should be even with the hip of B. Be aggressive. How many ways can you play the post? You *front, play behind, and side-guard.* When do you keep the post away from the basket? When you play behind. Do it the way you feel you can do the best. Now for the closeout. When the ball is passed to C, X2 must sprint 2/3 of the way, get under control the last 1/3, and contest the shot. X3 will sprint and front the block from the baseline side. X1 takes A. The coach makes a soft pass to give them time to get there.

DIAGRAM 3-38.

We allow B to turn and try to screen X2 as X2 closes out on C.

DIAGRAM 3-39.

Who's going to rebound weakside? X1 has the weakside all by herself. X3 boxes B. C passes to A or to B; they must shoot. There is only one pass and the shot. In the third phase, C dribbles the ball.

DIAGRAM 3-40.

Then we do it on the other side. Don't do it longer than six minutes because fatigue becomes a factor.

DIAGRAM 3-41.

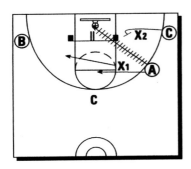

When the shot goes up, both A and X1 go to the weakside. C boxes X2; B hits and goes. If the shot is made and the ball is passed back to the coach, the players run back to the position.

DIAGRAM 3-42.

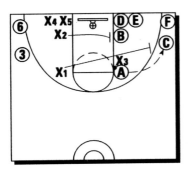

Now the shot is taken from the wing and on the pass, X1 will closeout on C and X3 side-guards A. X2 side-guards highside on B. Move when the ball moves. On this high-low drill, don't put the dribble in too early. You will have too many breakdowns. Allow two dribbles.

DIAGRAM 3-43.

We do this drill when we warm up. We go at 3/4 speed full court. Slide and run at the same head level, not bouncing up and down. If you get down too low, you have to stand to run. Just flex the knees. Slide, run, slide. A is facing the baseline. A slides left, runs right. The coach makes a pass to another coach. A will try to deflect the pass.

DIAGRAM 3-44. "ROPS." Rebound, outlet, postup, score.

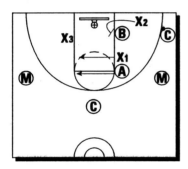

The coach shoots and misses. B rebounds and outlets to A. B posts up; X2 plays behind. A passes to B. B shoots. X1 boxes out. Whoever gets the ball, passes out.

There are *four* basic elements for success: *discipline, strength, endurance, and speed.* How many of you have a strength program? How many do push-ups every day? We do 15 of these every day. Lay back on your elbows with your hands by your hips. Come up on your hands and bring your knees to your chest. Don't let your feet hit the floor. The toughest drill we do is called "sidelines." We run the width of the floor, eight reps in 58 seconds. Over and back is one rep. We start with four reps and build. We go from side to side because there are more stops and turns. *Basketball is stops and turns.*

CHAPTER 4

THE MATCH-UP ZONE DEFENSE

BILL GREEN

The purpose of the match-up zone is to give you another look defensively. I happen to be a passive type of defensive coach rather than an aggressive type of defensive coach. I am sold on this defense. I'm not saying that this is the answer to all defenses; it's just my answer to defense. I believe in it that much. We will play it 95 percent of the time. *My defense is predicated on what the offense is doing.*

If you have a successful program, I believe you would be very foolish to change what you are doing. If you are struggling, the match-up may be the shot in the arm to get you over the hump. This is not a gimmick. There are a lot of coaches who feel that this has helped their program.

ADVANTAGES OF THE MATCH-UP

1. There are very few times when you are going to get five good players. The match-up will take the *slow, weak defensive kid* who can shoot the ball and allow you to play him. You cannot play man-for-man with inferior talent against superior talent and expect to win.

2. The match-up will help you get the most out of your team if they are not a quick team and not particularly *good rebounders*. The match-up will not work if you are sold on something else. You must give the match-up zone a chance and have some patience with it. If that is not the case, I suggest that you don't even put it in.

3. The match-up can *create confusion* on the part of the opposing coach, because he might not know how to prepare for it. It's something you can use as a *psychological tool*. Studying the match-up can help you prepare for it.

4. Another advantage is that it *takes the other team out of picks and screens* and puts them in a zone offense. I call it a zone because other coaches automatically say zone offense. That places us in a *1-on-1 on the ball with help on the weakside.*

5. It is better against a 1-4 set than a traditional zone defense. The 1-4 is an alignment that makes the defense match it. After the ball is passed once and one cut is made, they go back to a conventional offense with a conventional alignment. In the match-up, we don't care how you line up because we always know who we are guarding.

6. The match-up zone gives you a zone look when the opponent is running a motion offense and a *man look* when the opponent is running a zone offense.

DISADVANTAGES OF THE MATCH-UP

1. The match-up is not the answer to all questions. It happens to be my answer.
2. People will not spend enough time to give kids a chance to understand what they're supposed to do. Coaches must be willing to spend enough time and be patient with it.

RULES OF THE MATCH-UP

Begin in a 2-1-2 set because the offense will give a 1-man front. This will help on transition because they only have one man back. See Diagram 4-1.

DIAGRAM 4-1.

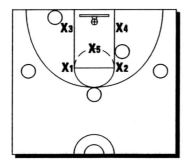

1. *Takes the point man or the man on the right with or without the ball.* This is a good chance for a little guy who can handle the ball; he is the key to your defense. If his man leaves, he will take another man and everyone else adjusts. He must always commit to a man.
2. *Takes the first man to the left of point #1.* This can be a big guard or a forward. He must be able to rebound on the weakside.
3. *Takes the first man to the right of the point.* This can be your weak klutz, a weak defensive player who can shoot.
4. *The rover. He takes the second man to the right or left of #1.* He must run the baseline. You will do a lot of talking with him during practice preparation. He must communicate with the other players. He doesn't have to be your best athlete, but he must be smart and understand the game.
5. *Takes the center. If there is no center, he takes the man on the right, high or low.*

Out of this 2-1-2 alignment, I can dictate what you are going to run.

DIAGRAM 4-2.

Following the rules, we have matched to a 1-3-1 alignment.

DIAGRAM 4-3.

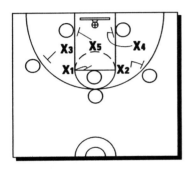

Against a 1-2-2 offense we match up this way. This contradicts our *rover* rule because there are two second men. But we use our center rule that says if there is no center, play the man on the right, high or low. X4 and X5 can interchange if a mismatch results; X4 can play *rover* from either side.

DIAGRAM 4-4.

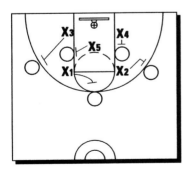

When they line up in a 1-4 alignment, we play this way. Basically a 1-4 is an alignment, not an offense. After a cut, it becomes a 1-3-1 or a 1-2-2. We bring X2 and X3 up by the high post to make them pass to the wing. This gives the weakside people a chance to sag and help. By doing this, the offense is more limited; this does not allow the inside people to go either way.

DIAGRAM 4-5.

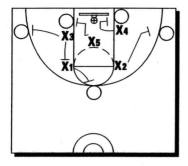

If they go to a low 1-4, all we do is bring everyone low. If they try to go 1-on-1 with the point, we bring X1 up and play a 1-2-2 to make them throw the ball to the corner. I don't feel that a 1-on-1 is the answer to beat this defense. If it's down to the last minute, I think this is a great offense.

DIAGRAM 4-6.

If they stack, we take X4 and put him on the high side and X5 is put on the inside. Whoever breaks out, X4 will take; whoever stays, X5 will get.

DIAGRAM 4-7.

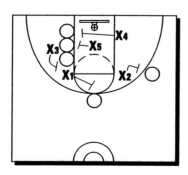

If it's a triple stack, X4 and X5 will be on the inside and X3 is put on the outside. X5 can cover out if they screen X4; X5 will be the *rover*. We are as flexible in our defense as you are in your offense.

DIAGRAM 4-8.

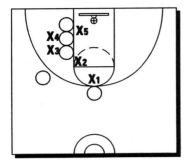

Against a triple stack with a wing on the same side, X3 would cover the wing first man right. and X2 would go close to the stack with X4 on the outside.

Anybody who breaks out right would be X4's man because of the second man rule; anybody who breaks out left should be X2's man first man left.

DIAGRAM 4-9.

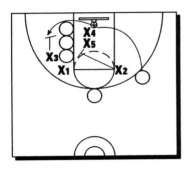

With a wing cutting under the triple stack, X3 will cover first man right. We do not want the ball to go to the stack or in the paint. We want the ball to go to the wing because once it goes to the wing, we can play helpside defense.

DIAGRAM 4-10.

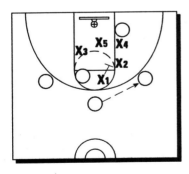

We will use man-to-man rules for sagging on the weakside. Against this 1-3-1 set, X1 drops to the high post, X3 drops weakside and is responsible for the skip-pass, X2 plays tight, and X4 fronts the low post. You are going to find that the offense will pass the ball seven to 12 times before they can get a shot if your kids are hustling. In high school, if they pass it more than seven times, it's likely they will make an error.

From this 1-3-1 set, if the wing clears and the point dribbles to the wing, you can cover it one of two ways.

    a.   By rotating around the center. X1 stays with the dribbler. If we feel that the point guard can score 15 points, then we stay with him. See Diagram 4-11.

    b.   By releasing the point man. X1 can release the point to X2, then X1 can take the weakside wing. X3 can pick up the cutter. If the point man is not a scorer and is not looking at the basket, then we will *switch*, as in Diagram 4-12.

DIAGRAM 4-11.   **DIAGRAM 4-12.**

DIAGRAM 4-13.

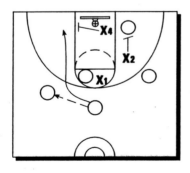

When the guard cuts to the low post, X4 will pick him up and X1 sits at the top waiting for a man to come up. If nobody comes to the top, X1 traps on the wing; they then have nobody to throw the ball to.

DIAGRAM 4-14.

When a wing cuts home the weakside, X4 stays with the post until the cutter gets to the corner. This forces them to pass the ball to the corner and not in the post. This allows X3 time to cover the post. Then we might *trap* the corner. We always try to *front* the underneath man and have weakside help.

DIAGRAM 4-15.

If the center is low, X5 can play low and X4 can play *rover* from the high post. When X2 or X3 adjusts, they would take the high post man.

If the opponents have a three-point shooter, play him man-to-man with X2 or X3. This makes X4 use X2's rule of the first man left. X3 still has first man right and X5 still has the center. It's like a box or diamond and 1. X2 will chase this kid no matter where he goes. X2 is not in the picture and not in the rules. We play match-up four against four. There will not be a second man left or right.

DIAGRAM 4-16.

Against an overload, we will send X4 to the corner if they don't pick him. If X2 can't handle the mis-match, we send X2 out and keep X4 in. Two ideas to keep in mind are:

Anytime they cross, we switch; anytime they flash, we play it man-to-man.

DIAGRAM 4-17.

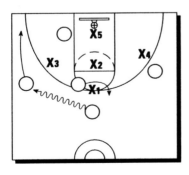

If the high post happens to be a guard and the high post steps out as a reversal man, he would be designated first man left and X4 would play the wing as second man left. I would not send my center out because I want my center to rebound. Post defense is more important than perimeter defense. If we bother a shooter in the three-point area, we don't think he can shoot 45 percent from there and beat us. We are not going to let the ball into the paint.

The installation of the match-up consists of 10 days for 20 minutes a day. We must try to understand other people—to try to have a knack for getting along with your players. Coaches must try to say the right thing at the right time. Because kids today have so many things they can do, if he comes out for basketball, it means he's interested in playing. Kids do not study basketball like coaches do. #1 could not care if #4 plays or not. To find out what kind of "team" player a kid is, put him on the bench. Out of this mind-set, I teach the match-up by asking this question:

To #1: *What can your man do?*

1. The man can leave, as in Diagram 4-18.

2. The man can *exchange*. X1 will switch on a cross or *exchange*, as in Diagram 4-19.

3. His man can *slide*. We teach both ways to cover this: to stay with the man or to release him. We may change it during a game. It makes no difference which one X1 takes as long as he has committed. See Diagram 4-20.

4. His man can shoot.

DIAGRAM 4-18.

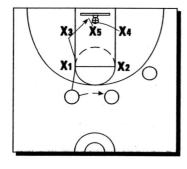

DIAGRAM 4-19.

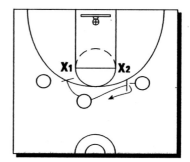

DIAGRAM 4-20.

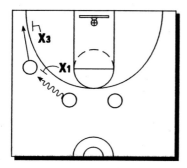

Then ask #2: *What can your man do?*

1. He can *leave.* If this happens, X2 picks up the wing or the first man left. See Diagram 4-21.
2. He can *exchange.* X2 will switch.
3. He can *slide.* X2 will go with him until there is another first man left.
4. He can *shoot.*

DIAGRAM 4-21.

Go through the offense you may face—2-1-2, 1-3-1, 1-2-2, and the 1-4. Then go to each position, teaching each one individually.

Sometimes we get too complicated; keep the rules simple.

Use the playing time carrot philosophy to let guys learn two positions in case of foul problems and substitution.

X3 can play X4 if he wants to play. We might sub at X3 and move X3 to X4 and X5 can interchange. We will *trap* in the corners to cover up personnel on the baseline.

We use man-to-man drills in practice with the 3-on-3 setups as shown. The defense must stop the offense three times in a row without fouling. We use the question of "What can he do?"

DIAGRAM 4-22.

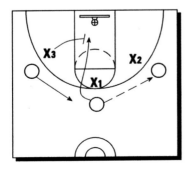

If the point goes through the middle, the wing comes over to cover. We use this to teach *weakside* help. If they screen, we switch.

DIAGRAM 4-23.

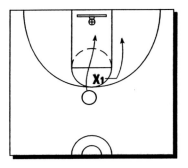

X1 will jump to the ball and deny the pass until his man goes below the foul line. Once he is there, he is not X1's responsibility.

CHAPTER 5

THE MATCH-UP ZONE DEFENSE

LARRY HUNTER

We use the man-to-man as our basic defense. You must have players with sound fundamentals. If you can't compete, you may need to use a match-up.

REASONS FOR USING A MATCH-UP:

1. Gives you a different look
2. It will cover up your weak defensive players
3. It will cover up poor match ups
4. It can be used with presses
5. Protects players in foul trouble

TERMINOLOGY

1. *Home*—your home base on starting position. Go back to your basic alignment
2. *Bump*—give a teammate a bump to get back home
3. *Cutter*—announce—call out
4. *Shooter*—Let them know where
5. *Vacate*—if the post is open
6. *Missouri*—Emergency corner-to-corner coverage if the post man is occupied. Play him man-to-man on the baseline.

ALIGNMENT AND RULES

DIAGRAM 5-1. "A" CALL

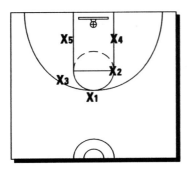

1. *"A" call*. This is a 1-2-2 look.

DIAGRAM 5-2. "B" CALL

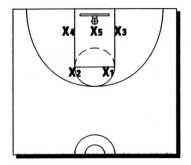

2. *"B" call.* This is a 2-3 look.

DIAGRAM 5-3.

3. Match off the point guard. Our point always matches to the right. Match from there.

4. You can play it.

       a. conservative—play basket area and only extend on the shooter

       b. deny ball reversal

       c. thumbs up—trap wing—thumbs down—trap the corner

5. Go through odd alignments with team.

6. The back men line up above the blocks.

7. Stay parallel to the baseline.

8. Do not chase the ball. Give the impression of guarding two people.

9. Don't guard the man in your area until the ball leaves the passer's hand—stay with man-to-man principles.

10. On all skip-passes it is the first man to the ball.

11. Don't panic if, for a pass, you are not guarding anyone.

DRILLS

DIAGRAM 5-4. COVERAGE AREAS

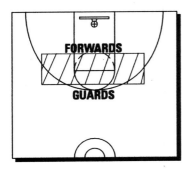

1. 5-on-5
2. Coverage Areas: This will show you the coverage area and how to get there.

DIAGRAM 5-5.

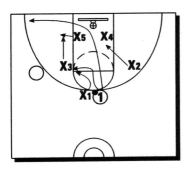

3. Stay until the lane on cutter in the middle gut-cut.

    a. You go inside/out after bumping

    b. X4 goes to the corner on the pass

4. The cutter goes weakside. The point calls the play.

5. If the cut is outside — it is easy to cover — bump and switch.

6. As the ball is reversed, they will occupy the post — call Missouri.

7. Weakside exchanges make for an easy bump.

8. Screen on the ball with perimeter players easy — switch.

9. On double penetration, penetrate and kick, someone slips behind into the gap.

TOUGH COVERAGES

1. 3-perimeter shooters
2. When a post player steps to the perimeter — step the defensive post out to the perimeter and then get a home call.

CHAPTER 6

BLIZZARD DEFENSE

JOE McKEOWN

We started playing this defense at George Washington because we really weren't very good. We had our real strong concepts of man-to-man defense and great pressure, but we were being blown out so we needed another way to play to stay on the court with these people. So, we came up with a match-up zone that we call *"Blizzard."* Since we have used this defense, our program has just skyrocketed. We have gone from a program that was 9-19 when I came in to three 20-win seasons playing national competition. This defense kept us in games against the better teams and gave us an opportunity to be competitive on the national level. I think this works best in the women's game. We play with a 30-second clock, which is not a lot of time. We control the tempo of the game and have a chance to hide a player who isn't very good. We can also take certain players out of the game. You may not want this as your main defense, but you can use it as one that you go to every now and then if you are strong in something else.

Basically, the *Blizzard* is a 1-1-3 match-up. This is the hardest defense we have ever had to teach because it won't work unless you have tremendous *ball pressure.* We play it from a half-court set and we nearly tackle ball handlers. It's impossible to run your offense against this when we play it properly. The problem is when one person breaks down, it is easy for the others to break down.

DIAGRAM 6-1.

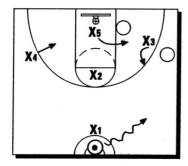

We put our two guards in line with each other X1 and X2. Sometimes we will change and put a 6' person at the top to create pressure and cut down on the passing lanes. X1 attacks the ball as it comes across half-court. Everything in this has man-to-man principles. X1 wants to force the ball out of the middle of the floor and this gives everyone else a chance to match up with someone. The wing on the ballside denies. The wings are interchangeable and the guards are interchangeable. We call X5 our *"hoop"* person, or middle person. X5 fronts anything low-post ballside. X5 even tries to front the mid-post as much as possible. X4 drops off for weakside help. X2 is our floater and tries to steal the next pass or match-up with anyone in the high-post area.

DIAGRAM 6-2.

If the ball is on the wing, X2 gets in line and X1 goes weakside, X5 is still fronting, and X4 gives weakside help. This is a hard defense to play against because when the ball is on the wing, most try to run some type of screening offense away from the ball. We try to match up with people as they come off the screens and switch automatically. There's no fighting through screens. But this is not a passive defense; we are attacking the ball, and we don't mind getting beat on the dribble because we have help from inside or the baseline. When the ball is on the wing, we're trying to force the ball toward the middle. And the defense almost looks like a 3-2 when the ball is on the wing.

DIAGRAM 6-3.

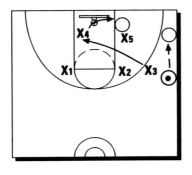

When the ball goes to the corner from the wing, we will do this three different ways, depending on who our center, X5, is. If she is immobile, we keep her in. If she is quick and agile, we will send her out to the corner and bring our weakside person X4 around and run the long slide through with our wing. So the ballside wing becomes the person on the weakside block. This is a difficult slide, but it is also very confusing for the offense because as soon as the pass is made, the person guarding her sprints away from her. Most people try to force the ball from the corner into the low post, and X4 tiptoeing the baseline. tries to step in the passing lane and steal. Remember, we have ball pressure by X5 in the corner, and we try to force everything baseline.

DIAGRAM 6-4.

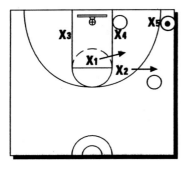

X4 is fronting on the low post, X5 is on the ball, X3 is weakside help, and X2 is denying the return pass to the wing. X1 is responsible for the middle-post/high-post area. Anytime we get the ball in the corner, we want to keep it there and shut the offense down. What kills us is when the ball is reversed. The things that really hurt this defense are *skip-passes and ball reversals*. When the ball is in the corner, we try to take away the next pass. We try to disguise this by making it look like a man-to-man defense, but it really is a point zone with one person on the ball and the other people adjusting to that person. It's really not that complicated.

DIAGRAM 6-5.

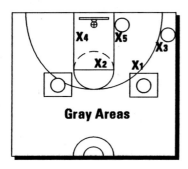

Gray Areas

All match-up zones have gray areas. When the ball is in one of these areas, you must have a lot of communication. Suppose X1 is guarding the ball, and the ball is passed across to the other gray area. X4 must fly at the potential shooter.

DIAGRAM 6-6.

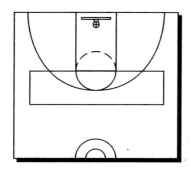

However, we try to cover the ball in this area with our guards if possible.

DIAGRAM 6-7.

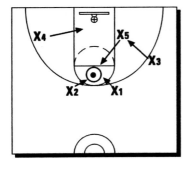

When the ball goes into the high post, X5 sprints and attacks the high post. Both guards turn and help defend when the ball is in the high post. It is actually a *triple team*. Most teams don't pass well out of a triple team and the person who flashes to the high post usually isn't a good passer. We are trying to deflect the ball. We try to make the low post look like it is open when it is not. As X5 leaves the low-post area, it looks open but it is being covered by the wing X3.

DIAGRAM 6-8.

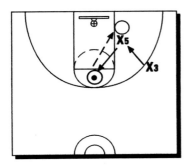

This is a breakdown drill that we do every day. Anytime the ball is in the high post, we drop both wings down and it really becomes a 2-1-2. We have a 7:00 a.m. running session for all players who miss the slides and the deflections.

DIAGRAM 6-9.

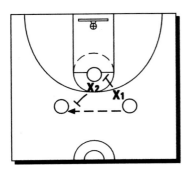

Another breakdown drill is for the two guards. It is 3-on-2 with one guard stepping in front of the high post for the deflection. We try to emphasize what will hurt us in a game and we can't let it happen.

DIAGRAM 6-10.

The short corner can really hurt you because of the pass out for the three-point shot. When I see someone open at the three-point line, I panic, because in the college women's game, the shooting is so good.

DIAGRAM 6-11.

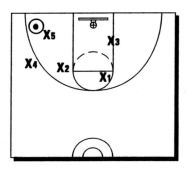

So anytime the ball goes to the short corner, the wing and X5 will *trap*. We try to take away some of their options. This is an automatic.

DIAGRAM 6-12.

When the ball is on the wing, we are forcing the ball to the middle. Anytime the ball is *above* the foul line extended, we *force* it to the *middle*. We will then trap with the X2 guard.

DIAGRAM 6-13.

Anything *below* the foul line we *funnel* to the *baseline* and trap. We run this defense several ways; we call them Blizzard 1, 2, and 3.

DIAGRAM 6-14.

For example, in #2, instead of attacking, she almost plays in between, because on the pass, she must cover the corner.

DIAGRAM 6-15.

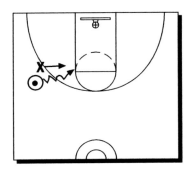

Normally, we are trying to force the ball back to the middle. We are really trying to take away passing lanes and angles. We pick up at mid-court for the pressure and to keep them from doing what they want. We want to get the ball on one side of the floor and keep it there. We try to get the offensive guard to kill her dribble, and then we gamble a lot. We have something called *"blue,"* and this means that we trap. We *trap in strange spots*, but that allows us to dictate what we want to do defensively rather than what they want to do offensively.

We trap the better teams. The better teams are so well coached that they want to make the next basketball play, the fundamental play. The good teams will throw the ball away before they will take a bad shot. Why? We take away the normal, smart play and make the offense make something out of nothing. The bad teams, it doesn't seem to bother them. Honest, we had a kid bank the ball off the shot clock this year and beat us. The good teams are so smart that they out-think themselves, and that's why it works.

DIAGRAM 6-16.

We trap with our wing and our guard when the pass is made from the top. We find that this is one of the best areas in which to trap. We are trying to deflect the pass. We don't even deny the pass to the corner. But we try to get a piece of it.

DIAGRAM 6-17.

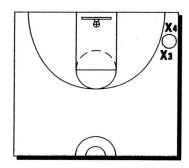

We call this *Blue Three and Blue Four*. If the offense has a great player on the wing, we use this to get the ball out of her hands. Sometimes we only trap one person.

DIAGRAM 6-18.

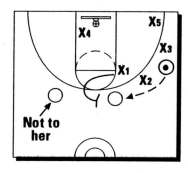

If we are trapping and the ball comes back out, we don't want the ball reversed, so X1 loops out to guard and tries to force the ball back to the same side. We don't want the ball reversed to the three-point shooter on the other side. Teams prepare for us in very strange ways. Before the ball gets to half-court, we run a 2-2-1 full-court containment press.

DIAGRAM 6-19.

We like to trap in the dead corner with X3 and X5. X4 tiptoes on the baseline and fronts. X1 will try to deny the pass back to the wing; X2 stays in and looks for the steal off the pass. If the ball does get into the low post, X2 drops down and takes the charge from the low post as she double-teams with X4. This is an all-out *kamikaze-type* defense the entire time that you are in it.

DIAGRAM 6-20.

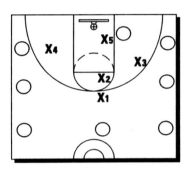

I want to cover the main drill we use when we put everyone together. This is an 8-on-5 drill. Sometimes we play it for 30 seconds, for 60 seconds, or keep score, with deflections being two points each, an offensive rebound a minus-two, etc. This gives the defense the opportunity to make their slides. We only have one person on the ball, and that person must call "ball" so that we don't have more than one person on the ball at a time. Work on stance and footwork, but most importantly, the slides.

DIAGRAM 6-21.

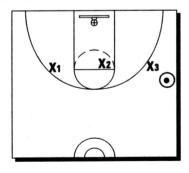

When the ball is on the wing, the guards must "get in line" with the ball, which means that they must drop to the line of the ball.

We don't have big kids. We had no post players when I got to George Washington. The first thing you must work on is their confidence. You must tell them that they are going to be a great player. That's the number one thing. As a coach, it is so easy to be *negative*. You must remain *positive*. I think that's the number one reason our post players got better. You must be realistic, too, and give them something to shoot for. Give them positive feedback. The drill work we do is geared toward making it hard, yet enjoyable. We have a name for every drill we do. First, we have the offensive drills.

CHAPTER 7

1-2-1-1 MATCH-UP ZONE

JOYE LEE-MCNELIS

When I first went to the University of Memphis, we had no one who could score, so we had to run the press. We spent at least an hour every day on the press, sometimes two hours. The only way we could score was to shoot short jumpers and layups. We not only pressed and trapped, but we trapped on missed shots. We were trapping every trip down the floor. Our kids did not really understand the work ethic that it takes if you are going to press. You must sell them on the press. We want to go get it. Not only in basketball, but in life. In today's society, this is important. To be able to press effectively, you must have an aggressive attitude. The players must believe in it, and you must be able to communicate. The press makes it a 94' game. It changes the momentum of the game, and it exposes weak ball handlers. We know that we are going to give up some layups, but as long as we are hustling, we are going to cause more turnovers and cause more rushed shots than we are going to give up layups.

Here are some *keys* for a successful press. You must set up quickly. You must communicate. In our press, several different people play several different positions. You can't come up from the back unless someone is coming behind. You must stay low, form triangles and anticipate. You must trap hard. The officials watch hands. Don't use your hands in the trap. Use your lower body. Make contact with the lower body and you will find out early in the game whether or not the official will call it.

Always keep the ball in front of you. Don't allow the ball to go over your head. If it does, sprint to the line of the ball. The back people in the press must always form triangles. Keep the ball out of the middle of the floor. Push the ball sideline. Ninety percent of all inbound passes are to the right side of the floor, so we cheat to that side of the floor. When the ball goes through the net, we have someone looking for their point guard. She doesn't look for the ball, she looks for the point guard. And remember, you only rotate up if you have back coverage.

DIAGRAM 7-1.

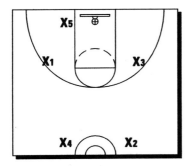

X5 is the least athletic player. The best athletes are X2 and X4.

DIAGRAM 7-2.

If the offense is a *1-4*, we will bring our people up. Our back people match-up wherever they are. In order for us to be successful in the press, we cannot play 2-on-2 in the back. We must defend your two offensive players with one defensive player. We must equalize that with pressure on the front of our press, 4-on-3.

DIAGRAM 7-3. DRILLS

Three days a week we run the front drills of the press and three days a week we run the back drills of the press. Every player plays every position in the drills. This is a front drill. X5 is on the ball. The manager is at the top of the key. X1 and X3 are wing players. We allow the ball to go in. X1 attacks and pushes the ball sideline, get ahead of her and stop her. X5 completes the trap. X3 is off the right shoulder of the manager. We believe that you can move forward quicker than you can move laterally. X3 is about a half-step behind. When you trap, we want the hands up, but the rear end down.

DIAGRAM 7-4.

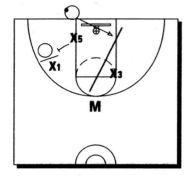

Now the ball is passed back to the inbounder. X3 must guard two people. We still want her behind this line (see Diagram 7-4). If she has to give up a pass, we want it to be the one to the inbounder.

DIAGRAM 7-5.

X3 will attack the inbounder and as the ball goes over the head of X5, she will turn and follow the pass and trap the inbounder. X1 will immediately leave. The hands are up and they point the toes toward half-court.

DIAGRAM 7-6.

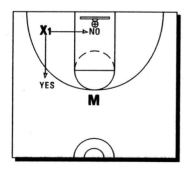

We don't want them to run directly toward the ball. X1 must head for the half-court jump circle. *Forget the ball* and find where you are going. Get a little behind the manager and then find the ball. We limit the offensive players in this drill. They can't dribble. We are working on the trapping. Then we allow the dribble.

DIAGRAM 7-7.

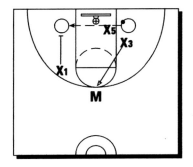

When the ball is passed back, the movements are reversed.

DIAGRAM 7-8.

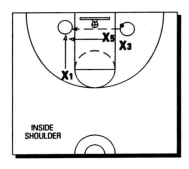

When the ball is passed back, X1 attacks the inside shoulder and pushes her sideline until X5 arrives. X1 cannot attack head on or she will be beaten by the dribbler. We don't limit the movement of the inbounder. She may break straight to the middle of the floor. We want X3 to be alert.

DIAGRAM 7-9.

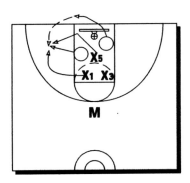

Another drill starts with all five players in the lane and the manager at the top of the key. Someone shoots the ball and X1 immediately looks for the point guard. X5 gets into the trap.

DIAGRAM 7-10. A BACK OF THE PRESS DRILL

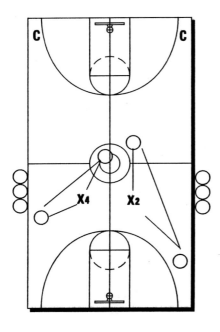

Run this drill on both sides of the floor at the same time. You need someone with a strong arm, so usually we use a coach to throw the pass. Each player lined up has a ball. X4 forms a triangle with the two offensive players. The sideline player can move anywhere she wants up and down the sideline as far as half-court. X2 is doing the same thing on the other side of the floor. The next player in line throws her ball to the coach and gets in the drill as the middle court player. The middle court player becomes the defensive player and the defensive player becomes the sideline player. The sideline player will go to the end of the line. We want to move the ball very quickly.

DIAGRAM 7-11. THE SECOND BACK OF THE PRESS DRILL

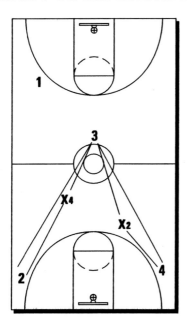

X2 and X4 set up in triangles. X4 defends 3 and 2. If the ball is on your side of the floor, you are up. The other person is back. Thus, X4 is up, X2 is back. They must communicate. X2 will call "back" even if she isn't very deep at this time.

DIAGRAM 7-12.

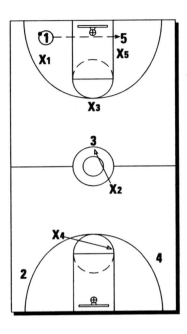

If the ball comes back to the inbounder, X2 steps up, X4 drops deeper and in the middle. The offensive players can move anywhere in the back-court up to the baseline.

DIAGRAM 7-13.

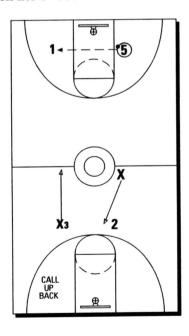

A *breakdown drill* which makes X2 and X3 call "up" or "back." The ball is passed back and forth between 1 and 5. You can't break up until your teammate calls *"back."*

DIAGRAM 7-14.

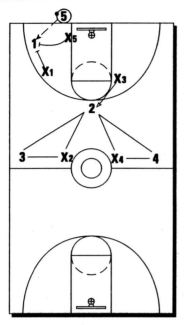

Let's put everything together. The ball is inbounded to 1. X1 and X5 are in the trap. X3 is covering 2. X2 is in the triangle, off the line. She is guarding two people. X4 is the back person because the ball is on the other side of the floor. She has deep responsibility even though she is almost even with X2.

DIAGRAM 7-15.

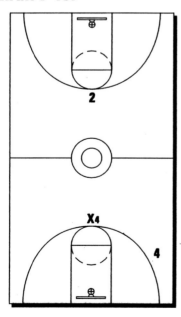

If 4 is very deep, X4 is deeper and to the middle of the floor.

DIAGRAM 7-16.

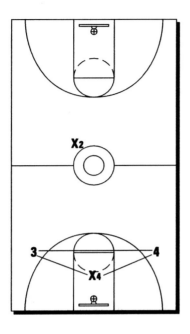

Sometimes a team puts two players deep. X2 stays near mid-court and X4 is in a *triangle* deep. This is the only time that she will be that far back. We will guard two offensive players with X4.

DIAGRAM 7-17.

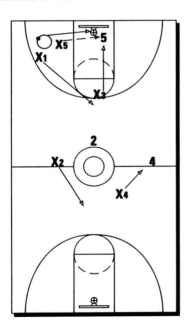

If the ball goes back to the inbounder, X3 comes up to trap and X5 goes over because the ball was passed over her head. X1 breaks toward the mid-court center circle. X4 comes up, X2 drops back.

DIAGRAM 7-18.

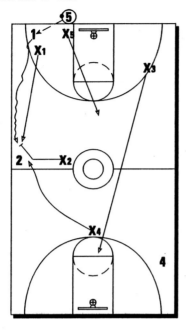

Suppose that *we get beat on the side-line*. 1 dribbles down the sideline. X1 stays on her shoulder. As she approaches, X2 is cheating a little more toward 2, knowing that she is going to stop the dribble. X4 is rotating up where X2 is. X3 rotates all the way back, X5 goes to the middle. X4 cannot go until X3 is sprinting by her or the offensive team will shoot a layup. In reality, X4 will leave a little sooner as she becomes comfortable with her teammates. The pass that the offense will most likely make is from 1 to 2. You will be surprised at how many passes X5 gets coming down the middle of the floor.

DIAGRAM 7-19.

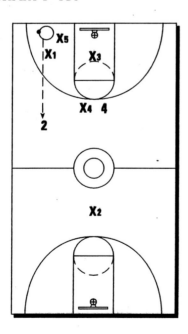

Keep the ball out of the middle. If X4 must give up a pass either to 2 or 4, the pass should go to 2. X1 should be putting pressure on 1 immediately. 1 should not be allowed to turn and look down court. X3 can also cheat down the floor to help.

DIAGRAM 7-20.

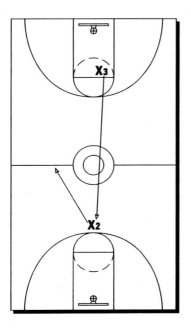

When X2 comes up to trap, X3 must rotate and take X2's spot. X3 must sprint. *We press until we quit pressing.* We don't have a rule. We get into a man defense.

DIAGRAM 7-21. DRILL, 1-ON-1

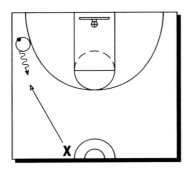

X must sprint to them, break down, and control the dribbler.

DIAGRAM 7-22. "HOLD"

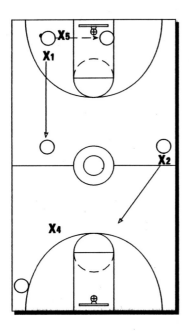

We do not attack the inbounder if she receives a return pass. We wait. We let the inbounder come to us or else reverse the ball. Then we go get it.

DIAGRAM 7-23. "DIAGONAL"

This is used when the offense throws deep. The difference is that they do not put a person in the middle of the floor. We change the front of the press. When the ball comes out of the trap back to the inbounder, X1 does not point her toes to the middle of the floor, but comes back sideline.

CHAPTER 8

THE MATCH-UP DEFENSE

DON MEYER

The match-up is based on our defensive rules. Any time the ball is between the circles, our alignment must be 1-1-3. The keys are:

- STOP THE BALL
- Tremendous pressure on the ball
- Closest man takes the ball
- Running to coverage areas
- Great close outs
- Five men rebounding

GUARD RESPONSIBILITIES

- Pressure the ball any time it is above the free throw line extended
- Work together as a tandem (1-1)
- Keep the ball out of the high post area

FOUR BASIC POSITIONS

BALL–pressuring the ball ABOVE the free throw line extended

WIDEN–behind the front guard in help position

HALF-WAY–when the ball is at the wing position being played by an up man, you are facing the ball one step out of the lane on the ballside between the ball and the free throw line.

CUT-OFF–when the ball goes to the corner, the half-way moves to cut-off in a deny stance.

INSIDE RESPONSIBILITIES

- Pressure the ball at the wing and below
- Keep the ball out of the low post area
- Help against lob passes

THREE BASIC POSITIONS
- **UP**–pressuring the ball at wing and below
- **MIDDLE**–dead front the low post man or area
- **HOOP**–help position that is one step in front of the basket

BASIC SHIFTS OF INSIDE POSITIONS:
- **UP TO MIDDLE**–the man pressuring the ball at the wing in the UP PO-SITION, on the pass to the corner runs to the MIDDLE POSITION as the MIDDLE closes out on the ball and becomes the UP MAN.
- **STAY CALL**–the UP MAN STAYS on the ball when it is dribbled to the corner, or when it is a short close pass to the corner. The MIDDLE MAN makes the call - "STAY."
- **MODIFIED UP**–when the ball is dribbled to the wing position and the guard stays on the ball, the inside player moves to a modified up, one step outside the low post area towards the ball.
- **UP TO HOOP**–when the ball is passed to the step out, the MIDDLE MAN closes out to the UP POSITION, the HOOP MAN steps up to the MIDDLE POSITION and DEAD FRONTS the POST, as the UP MAN sprints to the HOOP POSITION. Used especially versus teams that step out on the baseline.

DIAGRAM 8-1. BASIC ALIGNMENT

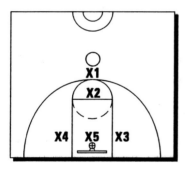

The low men start as high as the offense allows. X5 stays in front of the basket. X3 and X4 put one foot in the lane and one foot out, above any post men on their side.

DIAGRAM 8-2. INSIDE POSITIONS

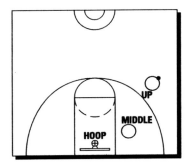

Up man on the ball. Middle — dead front post. Hoop — one step in front of basket.

DIAGRAM 8-3. INSIDE RESPONSIBILITIES

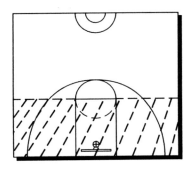

When the ball is swung to the wing, the area from the free throw line extended and below, is the responsibility of the three low men.

DIAGRAM 8-4. GUARD POSITIONS

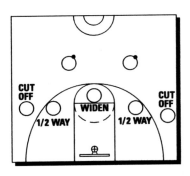

- Ball–pressures the ball
- Widen–keep the ball from the high post
- 1/2 way–one step out of the lane, facing the ball
- Cut-off–when the ball is in the corner, we are in a denial stance–a rear end toward the ball stance — cutting off the pass back out.

DIAGRAM 8-5. GUARD RESPONSIBILITIES

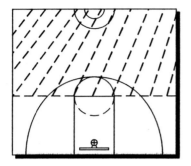

When the ball is above the free throw line extended, guards are responsible for the pressure on the ball.

DIAGRAM 8-6. GUARD POSITIONS

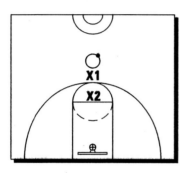

If the ball is on top, guards work in tandem. X1 is playing the ball and X2 is in the widen position. This is a rear end to baseline position.

DIAGRAM 8-7.

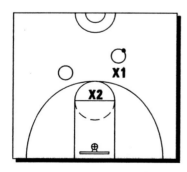

Versus two-guard front.

DIAGRAM 8-8.

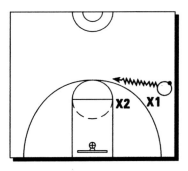

Versus dribble to the wing — the man on the ball stays on the ball (X1), the man in the widen spot (X2) moves to the elbow position and keeps the ball from the high post.

DIAGRAM 8-9.

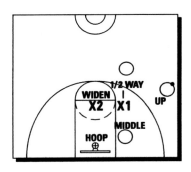

If the ball is passed to a wing, X1 moves to the 1/2 way position, one step out of the lane, facing the ball. X2 stays in the widen position.

DIAGRAM 8-10.

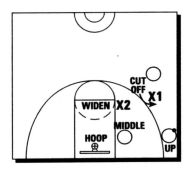

If the ball is passed to the corner, X1 moves into the cut-off position, X2 stays at the elbow and keeps the ball out of the high post.

BASIC SHIFTS OR SPRINTS FOR INSIDE PLAYERS

1. UP TO THE MIDDLE SHIFT

DIAGRAM 8-11.

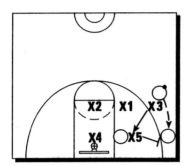

X3 is the UP man playing the ball. On the pass to the corner, X5 (the middle man) sprints to the middle position and dead fronts the post, X4 stays in the hoop position.

DIAGRAM 8-12. NEW ALIGNMENT

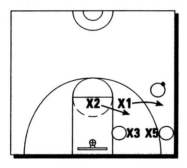

DIAGRAM 8-13. UP TO MIDDLE SHIFT (THE OTHER SIDE)

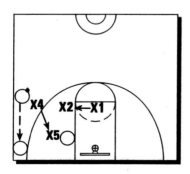

The guards are moving to their positions. X2 (who is the 1/2 way man) moves to the cut-off position. X1 (who is the widen) moves to the elbow to keep ball out of high post.

2. UP TO HOOP SHIFT

DIAGRAM 8-14.

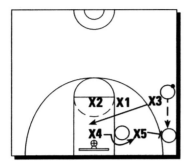

On the pass to corner, X5 (the middle man) sprints to play the ball in the corner. X3 (the UP man) sprints to the basket taking the hoop position. X4 (the hoop man) moves to front the low post in a dead front.

DIAGRAM 8-15. NEW ALIGNMENT

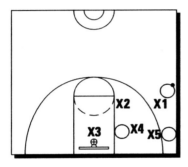

DIAGRAM 8-16.

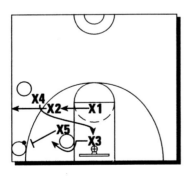

Up to hoop shift (the other side). The guards are moving to their positions.

DIAGRAM 8-17.

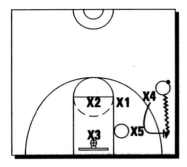

A dribble down. The UP man "stays" on the ball.

DIAGRAM 8-18.

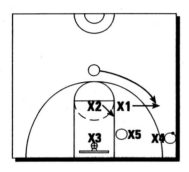

If no one is at the wing, the guard stays tight until someone comes.

DIAGRAM 8-19.

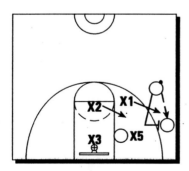

If a short pass, X4 (the UP man) stays on. The guards still move to their positions.

MODIFIED-UP POSITION

DIAGRAM 8-20.

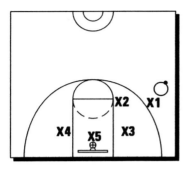

When the ball is dribbled to the wing, the guard stays with the ball.

DIAGRAM 8-21.

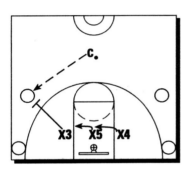

X3 is now called a modified UP — he is two steps up toward the ball, in front of the post. X5 moves to the front of the low post and becomes the middle man. X4 is the hoop man.

CHAPTER 9

"ROVER"
A MATCH-UP ZONE

DAWSON PIKEY

Why we use the match-up:

TALENT: If you play superior teams with inferior players, you need an unorthodox approach to defense. If your opponents have better skilled individuals, it is my belief that you cannot play these teams with a conventional defense. It does not matter whether your approach is man-to-man or a traditional zone alignment, the skilled players will be able to isolate the weak player into a one-on-one situation.

IT CREATES CONFUSION: Your opponents will be confused with what you are doing.

TEAMS MUST PREPARE: Teams will have to spend extra time preparing on how to attack the match-up.

IT IS NOT DIFFICULT TO LEARN: Introduce the defense in the first week of practice and it will fall into place quickly.

CONSISTENT: It is consistent with our philosophy of man-to-man defense.

HIDES A WEAK PLAYER: Teams with less talent usually have players with poor defensive skills.

FLEXIBLE: It allows for different setups to help disguise what defense you are using.

NULLIFIES OVERLOADS: Makes it difficult to use the overload principle in attacking zone defense.

COMPLEMENTS OUR MATERIAL: It allows for placing your best defensive players where their talents can best be utilized.

ALLOWS OPPORTUNITIES FOR PRESSING: Can press/trap either full-court, 3/4 court or half-court situations out of the match-up.

TEAM RULES FOR THE "ROVER" MATCH-UP ZONE:

- Keep the ball on the perimeter (deny the ball from going inside to the post area).
- Reception of all passes to the wing and baseline to be received outside the offensive threat area (normally the 15' to 18' marks depending on the level of competition).
- Deny straight line cuts to the basket from the strongside.
- Force the weakside cutter to the ball to go through an obstacle course. No straight line cuts to the ball.
- Cut off penetration drives to the basket.
- Increase the angle for all passes to the wing and on the turnover.
- Front the low post.
- The weakside player is responsible for lob passes to the post.
- Guards (key and guard) are responsible for high-post entry passes.
- All players are responsible for communication (when there are cutters-screens-lobs).

INDIVIDUAL SKILLS TO BE TAUGHT:

- How to read, to control, to anticipate and then how to react to the offense.
- How to pressure and to deny passes to the perimeter.
- The aggressive/physical game.
- Low post defense (slides/switches).
- How to contest cutters (strongside and weakside cuts).
- Defensive rebounding responsibility.
- Transition to the offensive end of the court.

INDIVIDUAL RESPONSIBILITIES FOR THE "ROVER" MATCH-UP ZONE:
KEY: "K" POINT – Position is with the back to the basket

- Responsible for designating match-up coverage.
- In a one-guard front – key has point responsibility.
- In a one-guard front – key pushes the ball to the right or left of center court.
- In a two-guard front – key has the responsibility for the offensive player to the right.
- In a two-guard front – key has high post responsibility when the strongside guard has the ball responsibility.

- In a one or two-guard front — key provides helpside defense for the guard and for the forward.

IDEALLY: Key should be tall with long arms and quick.

REALISTICALLY: Key will be your smallest player.

GUARD: "G" (Second Guard)

- Responsible for first man to the left of key.
- In a one-guard front — guard has wing coverage.
- In a two-guard front — guard has high-post responsibility when key is responsibility for the ball.
- Has help responsibility for penetration from the right or left of his position.
- Has weakside rebound responsibility when on the weakside.

IDEALLY: The guard is quick, agile, tough and an excellent weakside rebounder with size.

REALISTICALLY: The guard is our second guard or small forward.

FORWARD: "F"

- Responsible for the first man to the right of key.
- In a one-guard front — forward has wing coverage.
- In a one or two-guard front — forward pressures wing when the ball is covered by key.
- Has help responsibility for penetration from the right or left of his position.
- Has lob responsibility to help the post when on the weakside.

IDEALLY: The forward is the best rebounder and tallest player.

REALISTICALLY: The forward is the worst defensive player and a good rebounder.

CENTER: "C"

- Responsible for the coverage in the middle of the court.
- Usually plays on a line between the ball and the basket.
- Fronts low post player.
- Plays behind and to the ballside when post is high .
- Controls the lane line from the free-throw to the baseline.
- Prevents high post cuts to the low post area.
- Main communicator on all cuts .
- Plays ballside most of the time.

IDEALLY: Toughest and quickest of the big men.

REALISTICALLY: Biggest forward and most aggressive big man.

ROVER: "R"

- Responsible for the second man to the right or left of key.
- In a one-guard front — usually covers ballside baseline.
- Usually responsible for all strongside/weakside cutters.
- Has most baseline responsibilities when the ball is at the wing.
- Must anticipate the flow of the ball.

IDEALLY: Quickest player with size and ability to recognize the offense.

REALISTICALLY: The small forward or biggest guard.

BASIC DEFENSE:

- Weakside defense must always sink to the middle for help purposes.
- Weakside/strongside defense must communicate with each other.
- When the ball is on the baseline, the defense must sink to the middle and weakside defense will be inside the free-throw line.
- Be able to recognize double-team situations.
- Recognize rebounding responsibilities.

STEPS FOR TEACHING THE "ROVER" MATCH-UP ZONE:

- Introduce the match-up the first week of practice.
- Control all offensive moves.
- Start with the basic coverage and then move to the complex.
- Teach the slides with basic ball movement on the perimeter.
- Teach cuts from the top of the circle (strongside-weakside).
- Teach cuts from the wings (strongside-weakside).
- Teach reaction and help to the ball.
- Teach the slides for the turnover.
- Teach double–teaming/trap.
- Teach how to pressure/control the ball on the point.

DIAGRAM 9-1. Basic 2-3 set (Right)

DIAGRAM 9-2. Basic 2-3 set (Left)

DIAGRAM 9-3. Basic 1-3-1 set (Right)

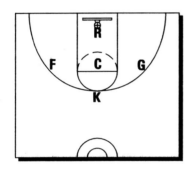

DIAGRAM 9-4. Basic 1-3-1 set (Left)

DIAGRAM 9-5. Basic 1-2-2 set (Right)

DIAGRAM 9-6. Basic 1-2-2 set (Left)

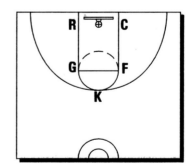

DIAGRAM 9-7. Ball coverage 2-3 set

DIAGRAM 9-8. Ball coverage 2-3 set

DIAGRAM 9-9. Ball coverage 2-3 set

DIAGRAM 9-10. Ball coverage 2-3 set

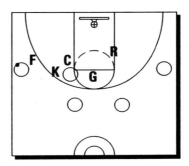

DIAGRAM 9-11. Basic coverage 1-3-1 set

DIAGRAM 9-12. Basic coverage 1-2-2 set

DIAGRAM 9-13.
Strongside Cut to Baseline

DIAGRAM 9-14. Coverage

DIAGRAM 9-15.
Weakside Cut to Baseline

DIAGRAM 9-16. Coverage

DIAGRAM 9-17.
Strongside Wing Cut to Baseline

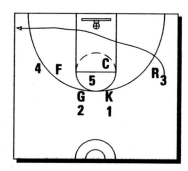

DIAGRAM 9-18. Coverage

DIAGRAM 9-19.
Strongside Cut to Baseline

DIAGRAM 9-20. Coverage

DIAGRAM 9-21.
Weakside Cut to Baseline

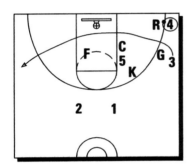

DIAGRAM 9-22. Coverage

DIAGRAM 9-23.
Strongside Wing Cut to Baseline

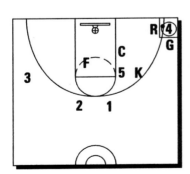

DIAGRAM 9-24. Coverage

CHAPTER 10

THE MATCH-UP PRESS

RICK PITINO

INTRODUCTION

The objective of matching up in a full court pressure situation is to trap the uncontrolled dribbler, thus playing the offense out of their strong areas.

The match-up press allowed Boston University to cause an average of 23 turnovers per game for a five-year period. By trapping only at opportune times, the defense stays clear of giving up high percentage shots. Furthermore, because we only trap the uncontrolled dribbler, the traps seem to occur randomly. As a result, scouting the press may prove frustrating.

The press is designed to match man-for-man on all movement of the ball; never allowing one man to force two defenders to play him in a controlled situation.

For the press to prove effective, maximum intensity is required. In fact, even the involvement of the bench is vital. Playing nine people is key to obtaining maximum effort. Non-athletes or weak defenders cannot discourage use of this match-up press. A mistake will cost you a basket in the back court area.

THE SYSTEM OF "BRICKS AND SAVES"

The system of "bricks and saves" has three major objectives:

- To help achieve maximum intensity and effort.
- To condition and reward positive actions.
- To condition against mistakes resulting from lack of concentration.

How does the system work? At any time during practice, a coach may call out a "save" for a player who performs a positive action. The coach may also call out a "brick" for a player who fails to exert maximum effort or makes a mistake resulting from poor concentration. (A partial list of ways to get "bricks and saves" follows.)

A manager keeps track of the number of "bricks and saves" each player accumulates. At the end of practice the manager determines the total number of "bricks" and the total number of "saves" for each player. Then the manager determines a composite score for each player. This is accomplished by figuring the difference between "bricks" and "saves." If a player has more "bricks" than "saves", his composite score is negative. If a player has more "saves" than "bricks", his composite score is positive.

What if a player has a negative composite score at the end of practice? For every *"brick"* not cancelled by a *"save"*, the player must perform the following task:

DIAGRAM 10-1.

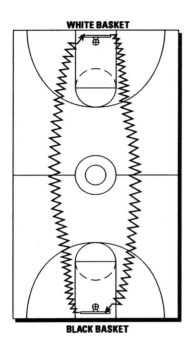

- Start on block at white basket.
- Dribble with left hand lane wide to the black basket for a left-hand lay-up.
- Dribble! Don't push the ball out in front.
- Keep your head up.
- Rebound layup and then dribble with left-hand lane wide to the white basket for a left-hand layup.
- The player must make six layups in 35 seconds. (40 seconds for centers).

  — If the player successfully completes the task, a *"brick"* is erased.

  — If the player fails to complete the task and the *"brick"* stays, time permitting, he will continue to go until he successfully completes the task.

- This drill may also be assigned to players from a losing team in a competitive drill or situation.

The players accumulate *"bricks and saves"* for 10 days, with the composite score of the last practice always carrying over to the next practice. At the end of 10 days, all players with more *"bricks"* than *"saves"* keep their *"bricks"*, while players with more *"saves"* than *"bricks"* become even.

We are confident that by emphasizing points like deflections, tipping from behind, and charges, this system is an important factor in the ultimate success of our match-up press.

Ways to get Bricks:	*No. of Bricks*
• Hands not up on defense.	1
• Not jumping to the ball.	1
• No hand above the shooter's eye.	1
• Not talking and pointing to your man on defense.	1
• Not jamming the rebounder.	1
• Missing a lay-up.	1
• Not blocking out.	2
• Not running wide in transition.	2

• Not running hard in transition.	2
• Reaching fouls.	2
• Offensive rebounder going over top of defender's back.	2
• Not denying the man in the lane	2
• Fouling jump shooter.	3
• Not seeing ball on defense.	3

Ways to get Saves:	*No. of Saves*
• Deflection	1
• 5-second count	1
• Block shot	1
• Tip from behind	2
• Offensive charge	2
• Steal	2
• Offensive rebound	2
• Diving for loose balls	3

The number of bricks/saves is subject to the coach's discretion given the circumstances.

PRESS BUILD-UP
DIAGRAM 10-2. ONE-ON-ONE QX

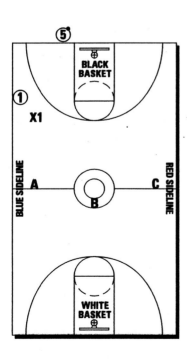

- A coach or player (5) takes the ball out of bounds under black basket. (Offense going toward white basket.) (Diagram 10-2)
- X1 three-quarter denies 1 as 1 works to get open. (1 must get open in area A below the foul line.) Trying for five-second count.
- After 5 inbounds to 1, 1 tries to beat X1 and score at the white basket.

  — 1 must stay in area A until the ball passes hash mark ii. Once the ball breaks hash mark ii, 1 can go from red sideline to rim to score.

- Do the same thing going from white basket to black basket and staying with area C.
- Discourage spin dribble

  — Sign of ballhandling weakness.

  — Vulnerable to traps and run and jumps.

DIAGRAM 10-3. TWO-ON-TWO

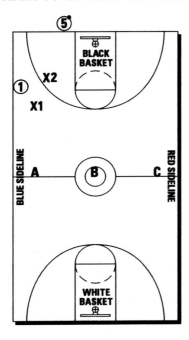

Defense plays with hands above shoulders and bent at elbows. (Diagram 10-3)

- 5 takes the ball out of bounds under the black basket. (Offense is going toward the white basket.)

- X1 3/4 denies 1 as 1 works to get open (in area A)

- X2 plays *"centerfield."*

- Once the ball is inbounds, we play 2-on-2 full court.

  — The defender on the ball works hard not getting beat.

  — The defender off the ball goes back far enough to see his man, but plays the ball.

- Whenever the defender on the ball is beaten and the dribbler is in an uncontrolled state, we trap the dribbler.

DEFENSIVE FUNDAMENTALS OF TRAPPING.

DIAGRAM 10-4.

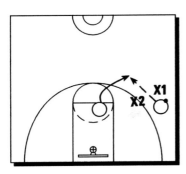

- The two defenders should form a "T" with their feet so that the offensive player cannot step through and split the trap. (Diagram 10-4)

- As the offensive player pivots, the defenders must move to *"stay on the ball."*

- The defenders constantly work to DEFLECT the ball.

- As the defenders work to deflect, they must stay in their own plane and avoid fouling.

- The defenders must sprint out of traps.

OFFENSIVE FUNDAMENTALS OF TRAPPING.

DIAGRAM 10-5.

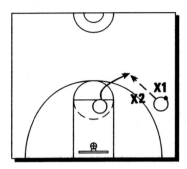

- Try to avoid trap by using a back dribble and then a crossover to change direction.
- Avoid spin dribbling! Spin dribbling invites blind-sided traps.
- Pivot actively.
- Take on 1 defender or try to split the trap
- Fake high to pass low. Fake low to pass high.
- The teammates of the player being trapped cuts to the gap that splits the trap.

DIAGRAM 10-6. THREE-ON-THREE

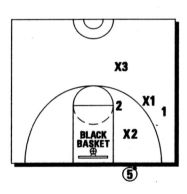

- 5 takes the ball out of bounds under black basket (offense going toward white basket.) (Diagram 10-6)
- X1 and X2 three-quarter deny. X3 plays "centerfield." (Try for five-second count.)
- Slides on inbounds to sideline, as in Diagram 10-6.

  – X1 plays ball and tries not to get beat. (Diagram 10-7)

  – X2 and X3 see man, play ball.

  (Discourage any pass, but play ball.) See Diagram 10-8.

DIAGRAM 10-7.

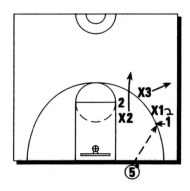

DIAGRAM 10-8.

CASE A: 1 goes by X1 with uncontrolled dribble sideline.

DIAGRAM 10-9.

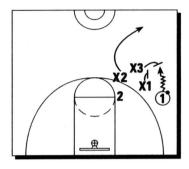

- Trap
  - X1 and X 3 trap the ball.
  - X2 sprints back, splits the trap, and plays ball.

DIAGRAM 10-10.

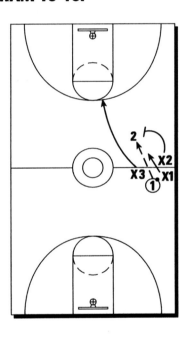

- Ball passed out of trap. (Diagram 10-10)
  - The trapper that the ball is passed over or around sprints out of the trap and tries to tip from behind.
  - The other trapper sprints out of the trap and back toward the strongside.
  - The third defender sprints back toward the middle.

DIAGRAM 10-11. FOUR-ON-FOUR

- *Man-to-Man* until the ball is inbounded. *Box* when the ball is on the sideline. *Diamond* when the ball is in the middle. (The same at all levels of the floor.)
- General deny area (try hard for five-second count)

- Ball inbounded toward sideline = box
  — The defender on the ball has his right foot forward, his hands above his shoulders with elbows bent, and he is pushing back.
  — The defender on the ball is not forcing sideline or giving middle.
  — The key is to make sure that the man dribbles rather than passes, so the defender is applying pressure on the ball.

DIAGRAM 10-12.

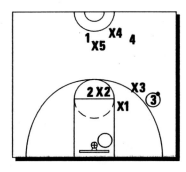

- The other defenders form a box. However, they back up until they see someone in their area. Therefore, depending on the spacing of the offensive players, the box is likely to be distorted.

DIAGRAM 10-13.

- Ball reversed back to inbounder.

DIAGRAM 10-14.

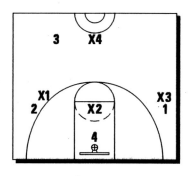

- Ball in middle–*diamond*.

DIAGRAM 10-15.

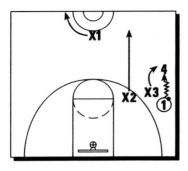

- Ball dribbled in uncontrolled state sideline trap.

DIAGRAM 10-16.

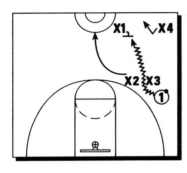

- Ball dribbled in uncontrolled state middle–trap.

DIAGRAM 10-17. FIVE-ON-FIVE

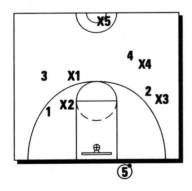

- This is a *2-2-1 press*, but it is *man-to-man* until the ball is inbounded. Then it is *2-2-1* when the ball is on the sideline and *1-3-1* when the ball is in the middle.

DIAGRAM 10-18.

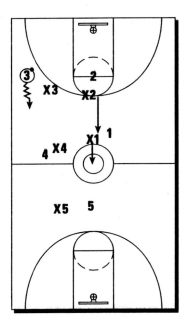

- Try hard for the five-second count
- Ball inbounded toward sideline. You are playing *hard man-to-man* until this point. Now you get into your *2-2-1* alignment with the center deep.
- The defender on the ball has his right foot forward, his hands above his shoulders, and he is pushing back.
- The defender on the ball is not forcing sideline or giving middle.
- The key is to make sure the man dribbles rather than pass. So, the defensive man is up on the ball hard telling the man to dribble by him.
- The defenders off the ball back up until they see someone in their area. When the defender sees someone, he stops. But as he backs up, he is always playing the ball.

DIAGRAM 10-19.

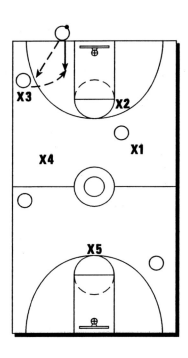

- Ball reversed back to inbounder, (i.e., middleman).

  — Most teams will come with a man in the middle, a safety valve, a man long, and a man ballside. They are looking for the reversal.

Here is where our defense changes. (Diagrams 10-20 and 10-21.)

DIAGRAM 10-20.

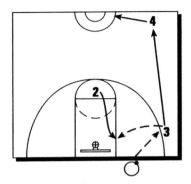

DIAGRAM 10-21.

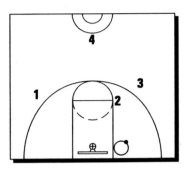

DIAGRAM 10-22.

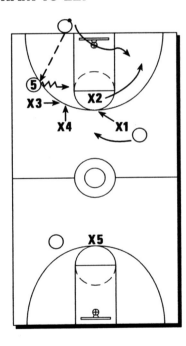

- Ball is dribbled to the middle. (The ball has been inbounded and is now being dribbled toward the middle.)

  — We are in a 2-2-1. (Diagram 10-22)

  — The offense will send the inbounder away, the man opposite would come middle, and the offense would be in a *1-3-1* set against a *2-2-1*. But when this happens against this press, your rule is to stay *man-to-man*. The other guard rotates right. The offside man comes middle and you are in your *1-3-1*. (So whether it is a pass or a dribble, you go *1-3-1* when the ball is in the middle.)

  — *Remember:* Play the ball, see the man. Hands above shoulders, bent elbows.

  — When 5 picks up his dribble, you rush him. Everyone else matches up and denies the ball. Most teams will not switch from their 2-2-1 offense even though you are in a *1-3-1*.

DIAGRAM 10-23.

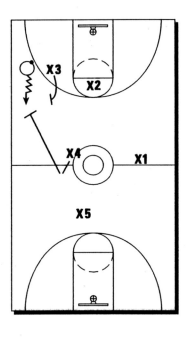

- Ball is dribbled to the sideline. (Diagram 10-23)

  — Most of the time the offense will bring a man ballside up the sideline.

  — If X4 cannot see a man as he drops, his rule is to drop only to half court. Even if he stops at half court, the pass will not be thrown over his head. (*Remember:* X 3 is on the ball hard with hands up not allowing the man to see.)

  — Because we are on the ball hard, the good ballhandler is going to start to dribble by the man. Here is the rule: don't allow the man with the ball to go by you with one dribble.

DIAGRAM 10-24.

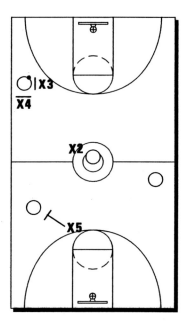

He must take two dribbles before he starts to go by the defender. The second dribble is the speed dribble. That's the one where the man puts his head down and does not see the entire floor. That's when we will come up and trap the man. (Diagram 10-24)

CHAPTER 11

THE MATCH-UP ZONE

ROY WILLIAMS

Let me give you two ideas, and you pick what you want. The first year at Kansas we played the point zone, strictly a match-up zone. That is what I'm going to show you.

DIAGRAM 11-1.

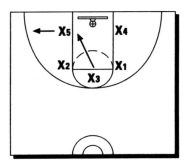

My second and third year we went to the *drop-zone* where we lined up three men at the top of the key and, when the ball went all the way to the corner, X5 would come out and X3 would front the low post. I liked this because we never had a guard rebounding on the weakside against the other team's big player. This year I decided we weren't hurt as much with that as by the 3-point shot. This year, we probably didn't play 50 possessions of zone all year. I'd rather be aggressive with a man defense.

Think of this. If you really love pressure defense, we had tee-shirts made, and it was an award. On the back it said, "When's the last time they ran their offense?" Because that's what I believe in defensively. So, after the first game of the year, I gave the defensive player of the game a tee-shirt. He was the only one in school who had that shirt. I'll guarantee you that the other players wanted one of those shirts. We gave one out after every game. I want to be aggressive. I want you to react to my aggressiveness. But if you are going to play zone, what scares me is the 3-point line.

DIAGRAM 11-2.

We will line up like this. When the ball comes across the ten-second line, they will see a 2-3 zone. In reality, it is going to be a match-up and we will match-up wherever they go. If their point guard lines up in the middle, X1 yells *"point."* He is telling everyone that he has the ball. X1 points the ball. Everyone has a partner. X1 and X4 are partners. X2 and X3 are partners.

When your partner points, then you have the basket. If X1 points, then X4 is under the basket. If your buddy does not point, then you are a wing. In this case X3 moves up, X2 backs off. We are going to have an *"airplane."* X1 and X4 are in line, X2 and X3 are the wings. The ball should see a 1-3-1 defense.

DIAGRAM 11-3.

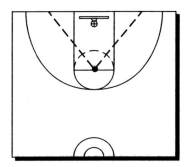

X5 must be somewhere on that dotted line between the ball and the basket.

DIAGRAM 11-4.

1 passes to 2. X2 points and goes out to where his toes are on the 3-point line if 2 is a good shooter. X3 is X2's buddy, so X3 is under the basket. X4 and X1 are the wings. X4 gets outside the lane, X1 drops back, and X5 is on that dotted line between the ball and the basket. We have the airplane again and we are in a match-up every time.

DIAGRAM 11-5.

2 now passes to 3. You must get your kids to use their heads a little. X4 is going to *"point."* But we don't need X3 guarding someone out of bounds. So, it's not an airplane now. X5 is still on the dotted line. X3 stays, X2 gets in front of the high post, and X1 gets to the weakside elbow.

DIAGRAM 11-6.

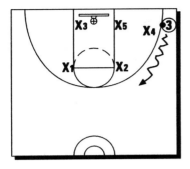

On the dribble, you must exchange the *"point."* 3 dribbles out. X2 initiates the exchange.

DIAGRAM 11-7.

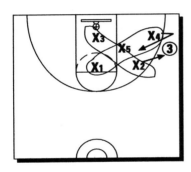

X2 rushes at 3 and yells *"point."* X4 backs off. X5 runs that dotted line. X3 stays under the basket because his buddy has the ball and X1 moves up and we have the airplane look again.

DIAGRAM 11-8.

Suppose the offense is in a *two-guard front.* 1 comes down and dribbles over. We have the airplane look again from the position of the ball.

DIAGRAM 11-9.

If they go the other way, the same thing occurs. X2 will take 1. We don't *match-up* our X1 with their 1 all the time.

DIAGRAM 11-10.

The one thing I don't like is this: If X3 is pointing, then X2 is rebounding on the weakside. We try to help this by also sending X1 to the weakside.

DIAGRAM 11-11.

Let's say X3 is pointing 3. If 3 dribbles to the corner, since it's on that side, X3 will stay with him. X4 will back off, X5 stays on the dotted line.

DIAGRAM 11-12.

It looks like this.

DIAGRAM 11-13.

If X3 is below the block, there is not room for X4 to come over because of X5.

DIAGRAM 11-14.

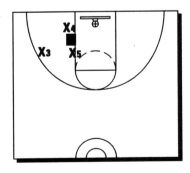

If X3 is above the block, then X4 comes over.

DIAGRAM 11-15.

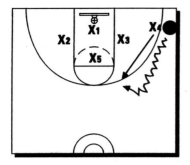

Georgetown does it a little differently. If you see Georgetown playing a zone, this is what they are playing, but if X4 is with the ball and it is dribbled out, X4 will stay with the ball all the way to the top of the key. X4 works with X1, so he must get under the basket. X5 is between the ball and the basket. X2 and X3 are the wings, but they are turned all the way around. I really don't like to do it this way. The *drop-zone* is a man-to-man when the ball is in your territory.

DIAGRAM 11-16.

If you have a zone offense that can throw the *skip-pass*, you have a good offense. We use X1 to stop the skip-pass out of the corner. X2 fronts the high post. But remember, we are going to cover you inside first before we worry about the 3-point shot.